"One of the most vexing problems that ca[n face] therapists is a dysfunctional family relat[ionship]. [Of the] many approaches to this dilemma, Dave [... solu]tion. It is clearly written and easy to follow. [... vignettes to illustrate] what otherwise might be difficult points to follow, and approaches the issue from a number of different perspectives. What I find most valuable about the book is the ability of a patient or non-patient to use it themselves. It can either be a self-help guide or can be used to accelerate psychotherapy. The book is definitely worth having in your therapeutic arsenal."

> —**James Reich, MD, MPH**, professor in the department
> of psychiatry at UCSF and Stanford Medical schools,
> and founder of the Association for Research in
> Personality Disorders (ARPD)

"Allen uses clear language and explicit examples to demonstrate an effective approach to dealing with difficult parental relationships (easily expendable to other relationships as well). Most impressively, this is done with a clear sense of the value of preserving these relationships and making them more fulfilling."

> —**George Stricker, PhD**, professor in the department of
> psychology at the American School of Professional Psychology
> at Argosy University, and author of *Psychotherapy Integration*
> and his most recent DVD *Psychotherapy Integration Over Time*

"David Allen provides an insightful framework to understand the lasting impact that critical parents have on the life of their children, well into adulthood. He describes powerful strategies to help adult children overcome this heritage. Better yet, he does this with a warm, empathetic attitude that is a healing antidote to the emotional climate of their upbringing."

> —**Serge Prengel, LMHC**, editor, *Somatic Perspectives
> on Psychotherapy*

"David Allen has successfully done what few academics can: write a readily understandable and highly practical book for the general public that truly has the potential to help those who come from dysfunctional families achieve more satisfying relationships with their families. With his uniquely scholarly, balanced, and integrative perspective, Allen offers many important questions and concrete exercises that will help the reader gain new understandings of why dysfunctional families do what they do, as well as how the reader can escape from those patterns and fulfill their potential without having to sever their bonds with their families. Highly recommended!"

>—**Andre Marquis, PhD**, associate professor in the department of counseling and human development at University of Rochester, and author of several books, including *Integral Psychotherapy*

"David Allen's book is an excellent guide for adult children who are trying to cope with difficult parents. In a clear and accessible style, he provides readers with a deep understanding of how children get tangled up in their parents' styles of relating, and explains, with concrete and useful examples, what children can do differently to free themselves from this emotionally tangled web."

>—**Gregg Henriques, PhD**, professor of graduate psychology at James Madison University, and author of *A New Unified Theory of Psychology*

COPING WITH CRITICAL, DEMANDING, AND DYSFUNCTIONAL PARENTS

Powerful Strategies to Help Adult Children

Maintain Boundaries and Stay Sane

DAVID M. ALLEN, MD

New Harbinger Publications, Inc.

Publisher's Note

Distributed in Canada by Raincoast Books

Copyright © 2018 by David M. Allen
New Harbinger Publications, Inc.
5674 Shattuck Avenue
Oakland, CA 94609
www.newharbinger.com

Cover design by Amy Shoup

Acquired by Ryan Buresh

Edited by Kristi Hein

FSC
www.fsc.org
MIX
Paper from responsible sources
FSC® C011935

RAINFOREST ALLIANCE
CERTIFIED

Library of Congress Cataloging-in-Publication Data on file

20   19   18

10   9   8   7   6   5   4   3   2   1   First Printing

Contents

Foreword

My client Alice had long felt angry at her mother and father. In Alice's childhood, her mother's self-absorption and her father's habitual stance of critic-in-residence had made the pair less than ideal parents. Alas, little had improved in her parents' attitudes toward her through the early years of her adult life.

Yet, as she entered her middle-aged years, Alice found herself wishing again that she had parents with whom she could talk, loved ones with whom she could share her joys and sorrows and hear theirs as well.

With David Allen's new book, the odds zoom upward that Alice will be able to make her wish come true.

Alice's desire to connect in healthier ways with her parents exemplifies one of the ways that human beings differ from animals.

With maturation into adulthood, a dog, cat, bear, horse, bird, or lion does not know, or seem to care about, the parents who sired and raised it. With adult ability to survive without the guidance of an elder, animals' parent-child bonds dissipate.

Not so with us humans. We tend to treasure our relationships with family members. We naturally seek to sustain those relationships, at least if the relationships have the potential to feel nurturing in at least some way.

It turns out, too, that caring for elder parents enhances our caring toward them. We love those whom we take care of. So as our parents age, renovating the relationship with difficult parents offers potential for major gratification on both sides of the relationship.

Dr. David Allen's approach reflects his belief in integrative psychotherapy.

As a leader in the integrative psychotherapy movement, Dr. Allen combines multiple therapeutic approaches. He masterfully interweaves cognitive-behavioral interventions designed to teach new thinking and communication skills with psychodynamic explorations into where the old patterns were learned. In addition, he combines a focus on individuals with a family systems theory perspective that broadens his focus to explorations of the reactions of parents, offspring, and siblings.

Study after study of psychotherapy's effectiveness has found that this kind of integrative approach to treatment most benefits clients. Readers of this self-help book can benefit similarly.

Dr. Allen took on an ambitious project in writing this book.

Can an excellent family therapist specify clearly enough what he does with his clients that readers then can replicate the process as self-help? I can relate to the difficulty of this project, as in writing my book *Prescriptions Without Pills* I undertook a similar challenge. It's not an easy one. And yet Dr. Allen has succeeded admirably.

Dr. Allen walks readers step by step through a process of reconciliation and renovation that has genuine potential for leading to the promised land of a loving parent-offspring relationship. With a voice as steady as the ones we hear on Google Maps or Waze, Dr. Allen guides you through the important process of relationship improvement.

Bravo, Dr. Allen, for this brilliant contribution to the enhancement of adult-to-adult family connecting.

—Susan Heitler, PhD
author of *Prescriptions without Pills: For Relief from Depression, Anger, Anxiety, and More*

Your Needs for Warmth and Acceptance

For many of us, our parents are a primary source of much of what is good in our lives. When we are children, they take care of us and meet our basic needs for food, shelter, and human warmth. They protect us and stop us from doing things that might cause us harm. They support us without overprotecting us. They teach us how to negotiate our social world to get what we want and need. They are a source of love and warmth that lasts a lifetime. We look forward to getting together with them to celebrate birthdays, holidays, gradua-tions, job promotions, weddings, and the births of our own chil-dren—or to being with them just because we enjoy their company. We think of them fondly, and when they pass away, we feel an acute sense of loss.

If you have picked up this book, chances are that these warm feelings are missing. Instead, you may well have a sense that your parents think there is something horribly wrong with you. Perhaps you experienced negative parental responses to the things you liked to do and were interested in. You may have felt that you were a dis-appointment or embarrassment to your parents in some way, or that your emotions are too dramatic or you are overly sensitive for their tastes. Their repetitive and compulsive negative reactions to your life choices, and the things you ask of them, may have led you to feel that they think you demanded too much of them, or even that you should do more for them.

Others of you may feel that your parents frequently act like children themselves, and that you are sometimes the only one in the room acting like an adult. In a way, you have had to parent your own mother or father—or both. They may complain to you about one another as though you had the power and duty to fix their marriage.

Perhaps you believe that, despite their seeming to love you sometimes, your parents do not really value you. Basically, your parents' behavior toward you is invalidating, critical, demanding, hateful, or otherwise dysfunctional. It is not out-and-out *abusive* (if you do come from a family that inflicts overt, significant physical or sexual abuse, this book is no substitute for working with a knowledgeable therapist). It is likely that not *all* your interactions with your parents were or are unpleasant. Rather, the unpleasantness is limited to certain times and places, or concerns specific life activities such as school, career, or dating. Their negative behavior is not ever-present; you may have noticed that your parents seem like good folks in other contexts, with friends and coworkers who seem to enjoy their company and respect them. You may have observed your parents engaged in pleasant interactions with these outsiders. Other people may even have told you that you are lucky to have parents like them.

Nonetheless, your parents are difficult with *you*. They *invalidate* you—meaning they ignore your feelings and ideas, tell you or others that your ideas are stupid or crazy, or claim to know how you are feeling as if they knew that better than you do yourself. They insinuate themselves in your life, taking it upon themselves to criticize the choices you've made or to dictate what you should or shouldn't do. Or they close themselves off and withdraw from your life at the times you need them most.

You very likely have tried to mold your own behavior to be and do what they seem to want and need, only to find that you were criticized for *that*. The demands they have placed upon you and the criticisms they have repeatedly leveled at you may seem to be inconsistent or even contradictory, putting you in a damned-if-you-do, damned-if-you-don't position. If you have tried, or continue to try, to "go along to get along," you find that this does not work. It does not put a stop to the unpleasant interactions. And throughout it all, their interactions with you are often a major impediment to your *self-actualization*—your living your life the way *you* see fit.

It is quite normal for you to feel that it is almost impossible to have a relationship with parents who engage in critical, demanding, and dysfunctional (ICDD) interactions with you without feeling belittled, devalued, controlled, criticized, betrayed, angry, or just exhausted. And yet you probably continue to yearn for warmth and approval from them, whether you like to admit it to yourself or not. You do not want to cut them out of your life, but neither do you want to continue to be subjected to their pressure, harassment, or outright hostility. You do not want to give up on them, but you worry that eventually you will need to either completely avoid them or resign yourself to putting up with their maltreatment. As an adult, you have probably questioned your own sanity for holding out any hope that you will one day gain their warmth and acceptance.

Because you probably have already employed many ingenious ways to improve the relationships with your parents, to very little or no effect, you may think it crazy to consider that you *do* have the power to stop your ICDD parental interactions. Of course, if that were easy, you would have already figured it out, and your efforts would have paid off. It is not easy. The solutions offered in this book require a great deal of planning and persistence. But you do have the power.

The Journey to Resolution Starts Here

Much of your family's behaviors have causes that you have no way of knowing about. Your parents' behavior was shaped by their pasts—by rules they grew up with, the way those rules clashed with their desires, and the ambivalence produced by having to live governed by rules that do not fit them. As I hope this book will show you, understanding these causes can help you fashion a series of interventions with each parent quite different from anything you have previously attempted. Once you understand what might seem inexplicable about your parents, it becomes possible to develop effective strategies for putting a stop to the recurring unpleasant encounters. This can be done once you learn about "metacommunication," which I define as how to effectively talk with your parents: that is, to talk about both the verbal and the nonverbal ways you and they react to one another and why this occurs.

You will investigate your family's history and the rules by which the family is supposed to operate to see how these rules create core inner conflicts in your parents' minds—conflicts that shape their behavior. Then you will learn how to get past their formidable defensiveness and denial about these conflicts so you can have constructive conversations about their behavior. The key to doing this is understanding and acknowledging those rules and the conflicts between your parents' personal desires and inclinations, and their own parents' desires and inclinations, which created a family value system that supports dysfunctional behavior.

In Chapters 5 and 6, I offer more than twenty-five strategies to counter your parents' usual ways of avoiding issues, as well as their ways of getting you to shut up about them. These strategies don't require you to pretend that you are not as angry or upset with their behavior as you undoubtedly are, and at the same time they help you avoid attacking your parents for who they are as people.

You'll also learn how to stop other relatives from subverting your efforts. There are ways you can request specific changes in your relationship with each parent, to address specific interactions and their invalidating, critical, demanding, or dysfunctional behavior toward you. Finally, you will gain the ability to address the unavoidable relapses into dysfunctional patterns of invalidating, critical, demanding, and hateful interactions between you and them.

This book can prepare you to have constructive conversations with your parents about your interactions. There is a lot of learning and planning to do before you begin metacommunication, so it's important, *before* you approach them for these talks, that you *read this entire book* as preparation. This is why I don't offer the actual steps involved in having these conversations until the end of chapter 9. I want you to benefit from seeing the whole picture first, so that when you do begin metacommunication, your efforts successfully free you from the family traps.

Where You're Headed with This Book

Effective metacommunication has much in common with what some psychotherapists call *assertiveness* skills (Alberti and Emmons 2017). These skills allow you to stick up for yourself and ask for what you need, while neither passively accepting whatever others dish out, nor becoming aggressive toward others, nor impinging on their rights and desires. The usual assertiveness skills often fail with family members, however, because these family members have ways to counter typical assertiveness strategies. Therefore, the skills you use need to be *tailored to the sensitivities of everyone involved* in order to prevent defensive reactions of fight, flight, or freeze, as well as any steamrolling or withdrawing strategies.

For example, if a parent offers unwanted and unsolicited advice to an adult child, an assertiveness trainer might suggest that the adult child say something like, "I appreciate your concern, but I think I know what to do." In relatively functional families, most parents would back off after hearing this. However, if a parent is secretly feeling guilty about not living up to some idealized image of what a parent is supposed to be, he might respond by compulsively repeating the same advice—as if you had not said anything. Or he might respond with something along the lines of, "You never listen to me, after all I've done for you! How can you treat me this way?!" or even, "What makes you think you're so dang smart?"

One important point: this book is absolutely *not* about your "fixing" your parents. They may or may not continue to exhibit problematic behavior with other people. They may continue to take poor care of themselves or avoid dealing with their ongoing marital or job issues. It is not your responsibility to get them to change any of that. Nor do you have the power to do that, even if you wanted to. What the book *is* about is fixing your *relationship* with each parent. This involves gaining understanding about and confronting the family rules and psychic conflicts that warp the relationship from under the surface. This allows you and your parent to learn to relate differently.

Repairing the relationship will clear the way for you to self-actualize—to live life as you choose rather than as your parents dictate. This is what is within your power to achieve. It is true that a discussion about the origins and manifestations of your own troublesome interactions with your parents *might* help them outside of their relationship with you. But this is not your goal. Your goal is to become free of the recurring interactions that stop you from growing beyond the painful effects of dysfunction.

In this book, I will share techniques and strategies I have developed in over forty years of clinical experience. Working as a psychotherapist helping patients with severe family dysfunction, I have found ways for them to effectively soften and address relevant issues with their highly defensive, difficult, and obstinate parents. I offer you a fresh perspective on and insights into why your repetitive and problematic family interactions take place, and how they came to be. I hope that this new understanding opens up avenues for approaching your parents in new ways. I am confident this book will be a valuable resource for you, and I sincerely hope your journey will be highly rewarding and empowering—and maybe even a little bit exciting.

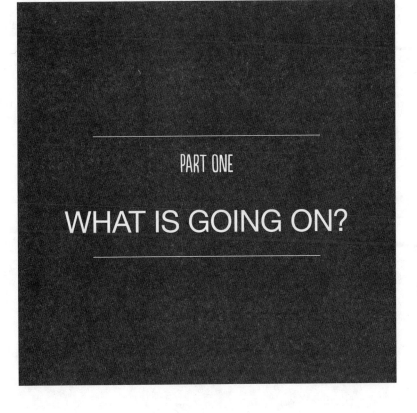

PART ONE

WHAT IS GOING ON?

CHAPTER 1

Ways to Understand Your Parents' Behavior

One of the main skills you will learn from this book is how—during the heat of battle, while trying to discuss sensitive family patterns with your primary attachment figures—to get yourself off of "automatic pilot" and transition into "manual." (By "primary attachment figures," I mean parents, stepparents, or others who had a hand in raising you, such as grandparents, older siblings, or ex-stepparents with whom you maintain a relationship. Anywhere I use the term "parent," please consider it an umbrella term inclusive of any of your primary attachment figures with whom you wish to improve your relationship by reading this book and applying what you learn.) This is not easy to do, since your family knows better than anyone else in your life how to push your buttons so that you quickly revert to your usual behavior. But it can be done when you have the knowledge I am sharing in part one of this book.

The first step in changing your problematic interactions with your parents is to understand them better. The knowledge you gain will set the stage for the strategies described later in the book, and it is absolutely essential for applying these without creating more problems than you solve. You will start by reviewing your current interactions. Then you will look at your parents' problematic behaviors in fresh ways that you probably have not considered before. We will discuss the rules by which families operate, which are shaped by a family's history and taught to us by parents or parent substitutes. These rules can come into conflict with what individuals in the family desire for themselves, which leads to the repetitive problems that you are having in your relationship with them.

This process includes concepts that may at first seem unclear or irrelevant to your situation. Bear with me and keep reading, because any confusion you may have will be cleared up as we progress. With any luck, you will eventually get to have an "Aha!" moment accompanied by the thought, *No wonder they act that way!* This understanding of the *hidden motivation* behind your parents' problematic behavior will inform every strategy for making lasting changes. It also allows you to hold in check your completely reasonable anger and frustration with them so that you can communicate with them with *empathy*. An empathic approach, as I define it, requires acknowledging their difficult dilemmas, but *without approving of any of their problem behavior*.

Identify ICCD Behaviors Common to Your Parents

The following examples are ICDD parental behaviors that have been described to me by patients and which I have also personally witnessed in my psychotherapy practice from otherwise normal, neurologically intact parents who do not have brain diseases such as Alzheimer's disease or schizophrenia. (With parents who have conditions like those, the strategies recommended in this book for countering ICDD behavior are not applicable.)

As you read through the following list, see if any of the items remind you of any *repetitive* unpleasant interactions that you have had with your parents. If a problematic behavior occurs only very rarely, it probably does not need to be addressed with this book's strategies, although this book will help you better understand it. Look for regularly occurring patterns of behavior that apply specifically to your situation.

Invalidation:

- Being negative or pessimistic about your prospects and interpreting whatever you say in the worst possible light.

- Telling you that you cannot take care of yourself, so you should not move away from them.

- Whining and blaming their own problems on you, or on everyone but themselves.

- Accusing you of being oversensitive and overreacting whenever you complain about anything the parent does.

- Calling you several times a day to check up on you to see if you are safe, as if you are unable to take good care of yourself, even when you have always done so.

- Taking credit for everything good you have accomplished, while saying everything you do that they disapprove of is "killing" them.

- Avoiding or abandoning you while seeming to consider a relationship with you annoying, boring, or unimportant, leading to extended periods of little to no contact.

Constant Criticism:

- Never accepting that anything you do for them is good enough.

- Criticizing and being obsessed with your homemaking skills, weight, hair, or parenting skills.

- Coming over to your house and rearranging the furniture and replacing pictures on the walls.

- Nagging you to get married or to have children or to look for a different or better job.

Unreasonable Demands:

- Repeatedly taking money from you while complaining how you never do anything for them.

- Demanding that they be included in all of your social activities, seemingly because they have no friends or activities of their own.

- Visiting whenever they want, sometimes unannounced, and expecting to be treated like royalty while never pitching in with chores or helping to pay for any expenses.

- One parent complaining to you about the other, thereby putting you in the middle of their marital problems, and seeming to expect you to do something about it.

- Complaining that no one helps them out, but either not letting you help, or finding fault with everything you help with—even to the point of redoing it after you are finished.

- When you return to a hometown to visit everyone, insisting on monopolizing all your time so you have no time to see old friends.

Hateful Behavior:

- Telling you to stay in an abusive relationship, or demanding that you leave a good one because they think they know best.

- Causing trouble between you and your siblings by gossiping about each of you to all the others behind the sibling's back.

- Showering you with unneeded and unwanted gifts while complaining about how poor they are.

- Spreading rumors and gossiping about your spouse to other family members or around town, thereby creating marital problems for you.

- Enabling siblings who do not take care of themselves, while ignoring adult children who have done well in life.

- Acting seductive with your spouse or romantic partner.

- Excluding your spouse or romantic partner from family functions without reasonable cause.

- Undermining your parenting of your own kids by going behind your back and allowing the grandchildren to do things you have forbidden.

- Making bigoted, highly opinionated, or gratuitously insulting remarks around your friends.

- Refusing to attend graduations and other activities with one child's children while fawning over another's children.

- Asking you to keep damaging secrets from other important family members.

EXERCISE: Recording Exchanges to See the Patterns

It is powerful to link your general observations with specific events. Ask yourself which interactions in the past have left you feeling angry, upset, disliked, criticized, or unreasonably controlled. Start a journal and write as many examples of past unpleasant exchanges as you can. Then ask yourself if any of them remind you of any of the behaviors described in the preceding list. What patterns start to emerge?

Part of what make the behaviors I just listed so frustrating for you—above and beyond their vehemence, their persistence, and the powerful ways parents prevent you from discussing them—is that they seem so damned inexplicable. *Why* do parents say and do things that are highly contradictory? Why do they care so much about, say, your following them in the family business when the alternatives are perfectly reasonable? Why would they go out of their way to annoy you by doing and saying things that clearly bother you?

When faced with maddening situations like these, you may have come to highly logical and reasonable conclusions about the reasons for your parents' behavior. You may have decided that they are just mad, bad, stupid, or blind; that they act this way because they are crazy, evil, too stupid to see how ridiculous they are, or simply unable to perceive the damage they are causing you. Alternatively, you may think that perhaps your parents are right and something *is* horribly wrong with you. You may go back and forth between blaming your parents and blaming yourself. While these are understandable conclusions, none of them are correct.

The behaviors that drive you to distraction do not come out of nowhere. No one is born to act in an ICDD manner. While dysfunctional family patterns are influenced indirectly by inborn tendencies, they are not created at birth. We *learn* social responses through our interactions with our parents. In fact, the human behavior that is most strongly determined genetically is our powerful tendency to learn this way. Our parents, in turn, learned their patterns of social interactions from their own parents, and so forth. Dysfunctional patterns often develop over at least three generations (Bowen 1978).

Behavior Comes from Attachment and Social Learning

When we humans first come into the world, we must survive a prolonged state of helplessness and dependency. As babies, we have no innate knowledge of any aspect of how the universe works, and we are completely helpless when it comes to taking care of ourselves. As we grow up, we stay in this highly dependent condition for a significantly long period, especially compared to other mammals. This has led to a situation in which we have all become genetically programmed to respond very strongly to our primary attachment figures—that is, the adults who raise us. Our caretakers are responsible for showing us how our world, and in particular our social world, is supposed to operate. Without that knowledge, we would not last long.

One of the most important things we learn directly from our parents is what our role is supposed to be within our social order, and how we are supposed to interact with other members of that order. Human beings are perhaps the most social of all organisms because we must cooperate with others in order to survive: we are dependent on the labors of other people who band together to bring us food, build our shelters, protect us from enemies who might attack us, and supply us with all our other material needs except for the few we can provide for by ourselves. The ways in which we are supposed to interact with our social group are, in a sense, burned into our brains during early childhood development—even if it means doing things against our own immediate interests.

Certain brain cells, in the primitive part of our brains called the *limbic system*, respond only to certain faces (Brothers 1989). They respond to only a mother figure or only a father figure and to no one else (Lott 2003). What we learn in the context of our early attachment relationships is extremely powerful and leads to our behaving habitually, automatically, and with very little thought in familiar-appearing environments. These habits are difficult to inhibit or alter even after we become adults.

We also learn to negotiate our world by paying very close attention to what seems to *motivate* our parents' behavior, as well as their reactions to both us and the rest of the world. One attachment theorist believes that by the time children are two years old, they are experts on how to get certain reactions out of their parents (Bowlby 1988). Of course, we cannot read our parents' minds, so we study their actions and their words, with the former taking precedence in making our determination about what they expect.

As we seek our parents' approval, we learn from them how to respond to social behavior and other facets of our environment within our social circle. Throughout the rest of our lives, we tend to do so automatically and without much thought or conscious decision making. If we had to think about everything we did during a typical day, we would not be able to get much done! In fact, we would practically be paralyzed (Eagleman 2015).

We have all inherited a tendency, under some environmental conditions, to give up our own personal desires—and at times even our very lives—for the apparent benefit of our family or social order. The most obvious example is the willingness of many individuals to die for their country or ethnic group in a war. It also triggers a strong urge to follow the family rules and play the roles that have been assigned to us, with severe anxiety resulting when we do not. This is known as *kin selection* (Wilson 1998; Sapolsky 2017). This tendency in animals was first pointed out by none other than Charles Darwin. We do not absolutely have to follow this propensity. We can choose to do otherwise, but doing so seems to us to go against our very nature.

Some of your parents' attitudes may seem bizarre, if not completely out of whack, because the rules and roles by which a family operates may have suddenly become obsolete and counterproductive due to changes in the culture swirling around the family. Your family may not have been able to keep up with the changes, remaining stuck with the old rules in a "cultural lag." Nowadays, these cultural changes can take place so quickly that parents and children may seem to be operating in different universes as they interact with the outside world in their daily lives—the children with their peers at school, and the adults socializing within their own social circle. When I grew up in the fifties, almost all the moms on my block were housewives and stayed home with the kids; if they worked at all, they were teachers, nurses, or secretaries. Just a short time later, women working outside the home became the norm. College women came home to their mothers excited about career opportunities, only to be told that no man would want them if they took that direction in life. The college women wondered, *Where did Mom get that stupid idea?* The answer: that was the paradigm their mothers had grown up with.

For most people, the balance has shifted between being preoccupied with the needs of their family and following their individualistic desires, a pursuit known as *self-actualization*. In Western cultures, in recent centuries, the focus generally has moved more and more toward self-actualization (Fromm [1941] 1969). Families stuck with old rules often feel highly threatened by personal freedom, but at the same time, may find it very tempting.

All these factors help explain why the behavior we have learned from our problematic parents is so ingrained and so powerful. This is also why your parents automatically react to their *own* internalized fears—which they learned from the reactions of your grandparents within *their* cultural milieu. When your parents seem most focused on you, often they are really thinking about *themselves*.

In the next section, I will discuss the nature and mechanisms behind *family homeostasis* and how it is enforced by parents, siblings, and other close relatives. This understanding will prepare you for what you will be facing when you follow my later recommendations for challenging dysfunctional parental behavior. Forewarned is forearmed; you'll need to have all of the various recommended strategies at the ready at all times—often when you least expect to need them.

Roles for Family Functioning

For any group of individuals with a common purpose to function smoothly—whether they be a family, a business, or a nation-state—all the individuals the group comprises must have certain roles and duties that the others can count on them to perform. In families, we can be flexible about such matters as *who* will bring home the bacon or *who* will take care of the domicile or *who* will bring the children to school, and so forth. But *somebody* needs to do each of these things, and do them predictably, so we all know that they will get done. We must be able to depend on others to do their jobs as expected. When that happens, the family functions smoothly and predictably.

Imagine that a couple's arrangement has been for the wife to always pick up their children from school every day, but one day the husband comes home to find that his wife hasn't picked them up. That would certainly be a problem for the children and for the school staff, who would need to ensure their safety while trying to contact their parents. But what if the wife unexpectedly confronts the husband for leaving all the childcare duties to her—when he has always had the impression she was content with this division of labor? This would throw all their assumed roles and responsibilities into question. The husband might well respond with dismay and defensiveness and be in no mood to start renegotiating each of their roles and duties, even if he thought doing that would be a good idea.

In families, the smooth, predictable functioning according to roles is called "family homeostasis." "Homeostasis" is a word borrowed from physiology because it works similarly. The body has mechanisms for maintaining certain important properties, such as an acceptable level of salt in the bloodstream. Extreme deviations from the optimal range can even be fatal. So, if the level gets too high, the body has mechanisms for lowering it, and if it gets too low, the body has mechanisms for raising it. Families have analogous mechanisms for making sure their members each fulfill their responsibilities.

The roles different family members are expected to play, as well as the attitudes they are supposed to have about various life tasks, are embodied and dictated by "family rules." These rules (which may at times be verbalized but are clearly implicit in the family member's habitual behavior) also specify when and under what circumstances individuals are allowed to bring up problems. They also dictate how much flexibility various family members have in renegotiating any given rule. Family rules tend to be followed implicitly and without question most of the time. Many families are able to update them or even renegotiate them to a limited degree under certain conditions, but other families have great trouble doing so, for reasons to be described in Chapters 2 and 3. The rules themselves originate from the norms of the family's cultural and ethnic group, as well as from the full range of historical experiences of the family group members, individually as well as collectively over several generations, as they interacted with the outside world. I'll offer an example to illustrate this shortly.

In addition to assigning roles and duties to different family members, these norms dictate behavior within a wide variety of contexts, including but not limited to:

- Marriage

- Child discipline

- Gender roles

- Sexual behavior and sexuality

- Social class

- Religious activities

- Careers

- Politics

- Responses to oppression and discrimination by powerful outsiders

- The pursuit of pleasure

Interestingly, families have developed their own version of theology to justify their family rules—referred to as "family mythology." It is sometimes expressed verbally as oft-repeated proverbs or sayings like "The devil you know is better than the devil you don't," "Nice guys finish last," or "That's what fathers are for." The shared ideas are accepted as gospel by the whole group, no matter what their individual experiences may have been, and even in the presence of glaringly obvious information and events that show the ideas to be problematic or even transparently false.

When Homeostatic Roles and Rules Are Challenged

Any family members who challenge a family myth, family rule, or their designated family role may be immediately attacked or invalidated by the rest of the family. When someone does not follow the rules, the rest of the family may gang up on that individual with multiple messages, all variations of "You are wrong; change back" (Gilbert 1992). Few people can withstand the onslaught of everyone they love and care about coming down on them with angry, attacking statements such as "How can you treat your mother like that?! Who the hell do you think you are?" When confronted in such a manner, most people meekly return to their former behavior. As a therapist, I found early on that I was absolutely no match for a patient's family of origin when it came to directly influencing my patients to either break with or continue to follow entrenched family rules.

When you attempt to discuss the family rules with your problematic parents, they may begin shouting family myths at you, as if you are an idiot who does not understand simple logic. But people use logic far more often to justify group rules than to establish objective truths (Henriques 2011).

While the rules of social functioning within our own family milieu are burned into our brains in this way, and deviations from them may be fiercely enforced by our relatives, I nonetheless believe we have both the ability to think about our own desires apart from the needs of the group and the free will to follow those desires. Cultural norms change and make family homeostatic rules obsolete; this leads to a phenomenon common to all human experience: ambivalence or conflicted feelings about the group's rules. To understand parental ICDD behavior, we need to look at what happens when a family member's own idiosyncratic desires stand in opposition to the homeostasis needs of the larger group.

Feeling Ambivalence and Intrapsychic Conflict About the Rules

When people feel they absolutely must follow the old rules that they were raised with, but they are sorely tempted to jettison them and enjoy more personal freedom, ambivalence results. Because those hidden desires often feel very threatening to both individuals and the rest of the family, they meet strong resistance; nonetheless, despite everyone's best efforts, they arise. The internal conflict between desires to follow our own muse, so to speak, and to be good team players in our families is called "intrapsychic conflict" (conflict occurring within the psyche or mind).

Of course, family members are not ambivalent about *all* the family rules, just certain ones. The rules most likely to cause intrapsychic conflict usually have become problematic through the entire family's past experiences within their culture as well as each individual member's natural proclivities. For example, some minority group members in the United States may have faced serious humiliation and violence if they attempted to assert their own rights to be upwardly mobile. They may remain afraid even after the threat has mostly ceased, and they can pass these fears on to their children.

Members of such a family can become ambivalent over their desires to, say, run a successful business, and in response, the family may develop rules about how successful the breadwinner is allowed to be. The rule is likely to be most restrictive in a family in which in the past, a member had been severely traumatized or even murdered. Furthermore, such a restrictive rule is apt to be much more problematic and conflictual for a family member who has a natural tendency to be ambitious than it would be for one who does not.

Since the original trauma and the resultant fears affected the whole family, the specific family rules that generate intrapsychic conflict in one family member tend to affect everyone else in the family: the conflicts are *shared*. For example, mothers and daughters often clash over the question of when to have children and how many to have. Specific issues like these are called "core conflictual relationship themes" (CCRTs; Luborsky and Crits-Christoph 1990).

Effects of Ambivalence and Intrapsychic Conflict

Fundamentally, these intrapsychic conflicts are what underlie parents' ICDD behavior. These parents subject their children to conflicting and compulsively expressed demands. They seem dissatisfied with, criticize, and invalidate their children's behavior when it comes to the conflictual issues. They even try to push their children and the issue completely out of their lives by behaving in hateful ways. Such parents are well aware at some level that they are driving you crazy, despite their appearing (and claiming) to be unaware, and despite protestations that they are doing nothing wrong. They may feel bad about it, but they cannot admit to their inner turmoil, for reasons I'll soon discuss. Here are some more ways their inner conflicts play out.

Contradictory Messages

Parents experiencing these inner conflicts often behave in ways that put their children and other family members in a damned-if-you-do, damned-if-you-don't position.

Distancing

When they are infuriating you, they may in fact be secretly trying to *get you to despise them* so you will go away and be free of their toxic influence! I refer to this as distancing behavior. This is very likely to happen if your parent was a "black sheep" in his or her own family. Such parents may later may feel bad about pushing you away, so they suddenly change gears and try to suck you right back in. They may even alternate between the two extremes, creating a yo-yo effect.

Acting

To appease our families, we usually have to appear to everyone as if we *want* to follow the family rules. Otherwise, we fear, they might start to suspect that we are trying to subvert them. To be good role-players without having to think too much about what we are doing, we have to lie to ourselves to some degree about our own intentions and motives. We can all be "method" actors, convincing ourselves that we really are the person who wants to do whatever our role requires. I refer to this as the "actor's paradox," because at some level, we must be aware that it is all an act. The actor's paradox deepens because in order to not think certain thoughts or respond to certain temptations, an ambivalent person *must* know what *not* to think and what *not* to look at. Hence, he or she must be aware of conflictual desires without seeming to notice them. Author Margaret Heffernan (2011) refers to this ironic form of denial as "willful blindness."

Secret Vicarious Pleasure

When your parents are paralyzed by intrapsychic conflicts, they are driven to keep at bay any of their impulses that run counter to family rules. Since parents often identify with their children, the parents may also be driven to stop *you* from expressing them as well. However, the situation is more complicated than that, because the parents also get vicarious satisfaction from watching you break rules that they themselves would secretly love to break. They may push you to act out their hidden desires and then criticize you unmercifully when you do! These conflicting or double messages make their behavior seem incomprehensible to you—and frustrating.

Doing the Opposite of Their Impulse

One way to identify family rules over which your parents are conflicted involves looking for certain desperate measures they may be taking to avoid letting anyone know that their covert, hidden desires even exist. A revealing marker for serious emotional conflict is based on a defense mechanism known as "reaction formation." In attempting to keep at bay any of their impulses to do things that run counter to family rules, and to avoid slipping up and letting people think they even harbor such impulses, your parents may go to extremes to act in ways that run counter to those impulses. They will compulsively *do the opposite*, no matter the current context, even in situations in which showing a bit of flexibility would seem advisable or important. They double down on the old cultural expectations and exhibit more and more of them. Their behavior becomes polarized. Polarized behavior is a big indicator of the major conflicts in your own family. If your parents seemed locked into, or compulsive about, behaving in certain ways, this could point to their underlying conflicts.

Core Themes Your Parents May Be Conflicted About

Your parents' behavior will begin to make more sense if you can figure out the hidden CCRTs that are creating it. The following is a list (Allen 1988) of some of the most common ones that can cause your parents to act at one extreme or the other almost all the time, or vacillate suddenly between the two extremes. With occasional exceptions, it's as if no middle ground or happy medium exists for them.

- Spontaneous versus planned activity

- Giving versus receiving

- Career versus family life

- Work versus play

- Emotionality versus stoicism

- Dependence versus independence

- Dominance versus submission

- Sexual expression versus sexual inhibition

- Caretaking versus caregiving

- Saving for the future versus spending for the moment

- Attention seeking versus remaining inconspicuous

- Taking all the blame versus blaming others

- Being responsible versus being irresponsible

- Competence versus incompetence

- Geographical and social mobility versus staying put

- Changing unhappy circumstances versus learning to accept them

- Togetherness versus allowing "space" in a relationship

- Ambition versus lack of ambition

- Loyalty versus disloyalty

- Respect for authority versus freethinking or rebelliousness

- Curiosity versus lack of curiosity

- Sociability versus preferring one's own company

- Prioritizing children's needs versus prioritizing parents' needs

While conflicted parents exhibit polarized behavior, they also give you double messages about how they want *you* to behave. They may make demands on you that seem highly contradictory. As described previously in the discussion of secret vicarious pleasure, for example, they may act like they want you to do something they would secretly like to do themselves but are afraid to, but then become alarmed when you actually do it—and criticize you for having done it. This damned-if-you-do and damned-if-you-don't bind is another major clue that there is a CCRT involved. However, keep in mind that all of us occasionally make contradictory demands of others. But if a parent exhibits this behavior repeatedly and frequently throughout most or all of your life, it's a clear indicator of an important CCRT.

EXERCISE: Identifying Polarities and Double Messages

As you look over the preceding list of polarities, are there issues you recognize as ones in which your parents mostly act at one extreme or the other in a compulsive manner, or inexplicably vacillate from one extreme to the other? Also, think about whether you have been frequently criticized for being for being too much one way or too much the other. Review your history with your parents for evidence of polarized behavior, contradictory demands, and ICDD interactions. Record your observations in your journal.

Another useful source of information about your parents' CCRTs, as you've observed them in various contexts, is their *attitudes* about certain behaviors exhibited by you and others. This exercise helps identify the issues behind your parents' important *polarized* or *contradictory* behavior toward you (Allen et al. 2005). A list of nine behavior domains is followed by a detailed inventory of behaviors that fall within each domain. As you read through the behaviors, you'll record any that match your experience with each of your parents.

Behavior Domains:

1. Praise and criticism

2. Comments about you to friends and relatives

3. How the person seems to react to whether you follow the advice offered

4. Who the person blames for the person's problems

5. How often the person gives you advice about specific life issues

6. How preoccupied the person is with you and what you do about certain life goals

7. How the person's mood relates to your mood

8. The person's reactions to your career failures and successes

9. The person's reactions to your romantic failures and successes

As you read through the following detailed inventory of specific behaviors, for each of the nine domains, choose the one option listed that describes the parent's behavior toward you the *majority of the time* when it comes to problematic interactions. Keep in mind that there will always be times when the parent does not show that attitude, or even times when the parent behaves in an exactly opposite manner, because that is the nature of ambivalence. Note: For each domain, the first two options represent polarized behavior, the third and the last represent double messages, and the fourth represents nonconflictual behavior. The fifth item represents compulsive avoidance of an issue—another indication of ambivalence about it. There is one additional option for domain 4 only (behavior 6), a variation of nonconflictual behavior.

Domain 1. Praise and criticism

1. This person consistently praises me, no matter how I decide to run some specific aspect of my life.

2. This person consistently criticizes me, no matter how I decide to run some specific aspect of my life.

3. This person consistently goes back and forth between praising and criticizing me over the same specific decisions.

4. This person is consistently fair in praising or criticizing me for my decisions.

5. This person rarely praises or criticizes my decisions about how I run my life.

6. This person consistently says one thing but really means another when responding to my specific life decisions.

Domain 2. Comments to friends and relatives about you

1. This person consistently brags to friends and relatives about certain things I've done.

2. This person consistently badmouths me to friends and relatives about certain things I've done.

3. This person says contradictory things to friends and relatives about certain things I've done.

4. This person is consistently fair in making remarks about me to friends and relatives.

5. This person consistently does not talk about me with their friends and relatives.

6. This person consistently says one thing about me to friends and relatives but really means another.

Domain 3. How the person seems to react to whether you follow the person's advice

1. This person acts happy only if I follow his advice about certain life issues.

2. This person acts happy only if I ignore his advice about certain life issues.

3. This person consistently acts unhappy with my reaction to his advice about certain life issues, no matter whether I follow or ignore it.

4. This person accepts my reaction to his advice even if I disagree with it.

5. This person consistently does not react to how I respond to his advice.

6. This person consistently acts one way but really feels another when responding to my reactions to his advice about certain life issues.

Domain 4. Who the person blames for specific problems

1. This person consistently blames herself for a problem she has even when he is not at fault.

2. This person consistently blames me for a problem she has even when I'm not at fault.

3. This person consistently goes back and forth between blaming me and herself for a problem she has.

4. This person is fair in assigning blame for her problems.

5. This person consistently blames others rather than me or herself for a problem she has.

6. This person rarely blames anyone for her own problems.

7. This person consistently says one thing but means another when assigning blame for a problem she has.

Domain 5. How often the person gives you advice about specific life issues

1. This person almost never tells me what to do about specific life issues, even if I ask for her advice.

2. This person almost always tells me what to do about specific life issues.

3. This person consistently goes back and forth between telling me to make my own decisions and telling me what to do about specific life issues.

4. This person usually tells me to make my own independent decisions but will offer advice if asked.

5. This person is unconcerned with who makes the decisions in my life.

6. This person consistently says one thing but really means another when it comes to telling me what to do about specific life issues.

Domain 6. How preoccupied the person is with you and what you do about certain life goals

1. This person consistently expresses worries about how I am doing when I am engaged in certain pursuits, even when she knows I'm doing well.

2. This person never expresses worries about me when I am engaged in certain pursuits, even when he knows I'm in trouble.

3. This person goes back and forth between expressing worry and saying nothing about how I'm doing when I am engaged in certain pursuits.

4. This person is consistently reasonable when expressing concerns about how I'm doing.

5. This person doesn't even bother to find out how I am doing when I am engaged in certain pursuits.

6. This person consistently says one thing but really means another in terms of worrying about how I'm doing when I am engaged in certain pursuits.

Domain 7. How the person's mood relates to your mood

1. This person acts happy only when I am happy.

2. This person acts happy only when I am miserable.

3. This person goes back and forth between acting happy when I'm happy and acting happy when I'm miserable.

4. This person shows sympathy with how I feel, but her mood does not depend on how I am feeling.

5. This person almost never reacts to how I am feeling.

6. This person consistently acts one way but really feels another way when I'm happy or unhappy.

Domain 8. The person's reactions to your career failures and successes

1. This person does not act happy unless I am succeeding in my career.

2. This person usually acts unhappy about my career accomplishments and relishes my failures.

3. This person goes back and forth between acting happy about my career successes and relishing my failures.

4. This person expresses satisfaction with my career successes and sympathizes with my career failures.

5. This person almost never reacts to my career successes and failures.

6. This person consistently acts one way but really feels another way when reacting to my career successes and failures.

Domain 9. The person's reactions to your romantic failures and successes

1. This person does not act happy unless I am having a successful romantic relationship.

2. This person usually acts unhappy about my successes in romantic relationships and relishes my romantic failures.

3. This person goes back and forth between being happy about my romantic successes and relishing my romantic failures.

4. This person expresses satisfaction with my romantic successes and sympathizes with my romantic failures.

5. This person consistently does not react to how I am doing in romantic relationships.

6. This person consistently acts one way but really feels another when reacting to my love life.

For any domains in which contradictory, polarized, or back-and-forth (from one extreme to the other) behavior is the norm, write in your journal about the times when each parent has engaged in this particular behavior. Ask yourself:

•   What was going on with me and with the person at the time?

•   What was the subject of, say, his praise or criticism?

•   What specifically did I do that seemed to affect her mood?

Did the behavior have to do with, for example, whether you were being spontaneous or highly regimented, what you gave to someone, or the help you received from someone? Writing about this will help you get closer to identifying what CCRT the parent is having a problem with, and also its specific manifestation.

Observing Your Parents' Inner Conflicts

The next step is to start observing the interactions between you and your parents in the present. Carefully watch *all* of your parents' behavior during those times in which they exhibit evidence of internal conflicts. Observations are also useful when, if you even allude to how you feel about their behavior or the situations in which it usually occurs, they seem to be acting defensively or with hostile responses to you. I recommend that you start watching the behavior of both your problematic family members as well as your own during these difficult exchanges. As you do this, *do not try to fix or change anything.* Just watch.

Look at their behavior before, while, and after they exhibit any of the repetitive ICDD behaviors. Then, as soon as no one is around to observe you, write down the conversations that took place, as close to verbatim as you can recall. Describe any behavior that accompanied them. Be sure you write everything in chronological order, paying particular attention to how the conversations *got started* and how they *ended.*

Be very specific in your behavioral descriptions. Keep in mind that someone cannot just "not react at all." Staring blankly at the ceiling is, in fact, a reaction. Particularly important for future reference is any series of reactions or responses that seem to frequently recur in your family. Your observations in this regard will provide clues as to which family conflictual issues may be operating.

Identifying the issues with which your parents struggle will help guide you in your next step in putting a stop to dysfunctional interactions: investigating the family history that drove the family to create the problematic rules under which they operate in the first place. This understanding will in turn help you approach them in a constructive, effective problem-solving manner. But first, I will address one additional consideration: understanding—and being able to acknowledge—how you have been interpreting and reacting to their behavior. In the next chapter, we will look closely at how the children of conflicted and ambivalent parents tend to respond to them in an effort to manage their parents' apparent instability.

CHAPTER 2

How Have You Been Responding?

What comes next may be difficult: you're going to look at your own responses to your parents' problematic behavior and what you may be trying to accomplish by reacting as you do. Importantly, the point is definitely not to make you feel deserving of blame or guilty—in fact, just the opposite. Although you need to take responsibility for your own behavior when it comes time to confront the dysfunctional patterns, you nonetheless have very good and understandable reasons for behaving as you have been. You've done what was best, given what you were observing and what you knew.

Because your impulse to follow a different path than the one dictated by family rules remains present, despite efforts to defend it or hide it, when the issues that your parents are conflicted about arise, your parents often appear to become unstable. When parents become unstable, this in turn destabilizes the whole family, because parents are the leaders of the family group. If you see this, you may begin to fear that your parents might completely lose it and have a mental breakdown, get depressed and nonfunctional, start drinking too much, or abandon each other or even the whole family.

In this situation, it's natural for you to do your best to try to stabilize your parents by whatever means necessary—even at great personal cost to yourself. Because you cannot read minds, you do not understand what is really motivating your parents to act in the unstable ways they do. You can only guess. Nonetheless, you quickly figure out how to behave in order to *temporarily* fix things.

EXERCISE: How Do You Respond to Your Parents' ICDD Behavior?

Review the results of the previous exercise, "Identifying Polarities and Double Messages," and think back over the ICDD behaviors that your parents have exhibited with you. Think about how you tend to respond. Ask yourself how you may have tried to placate your parents and whether you may have been either subtly rewarded or subtly punished for your responses. Then look at the bigger picture: How has your life been limited by your parents' dysfunction, both in your childhood and in the present? What has it cost you? How has it made your self-actualization impossible? Write down your thoughts on these questions.

While the behavior patterns that you may have developed to help stabilize your conflicted parents work over the short term, in the long run, they not only are self-defeating for you, but also actually *worsen* your family problems over time. If people act out problems instead of talking them out, everyone avoids directly addressing their problems—and finding solutions for them. Problems that cannot be discussed cannot be solved! Temporary "solutions" are nonetheless powerful precisely because when you employ them, things get better before they get worse. There is often a significant time lag before they get worse, which masks how counterproductive they are.

Let's look at the ways in which children and adult children attempt to stabilize unstable parents. This is not a complete list, but it describes patterns I have most commonly observed. As you read through these, ask yourself if any of them ring a bell for you and apply to how you have dealt with your parents.

Partially Expressing Parents' Repressed Impulses

Parents often live vicariously through their children. It is not just "stage mothers" and the like who overidentify with their children; almost every parent does it to some extent. This process creates problems when these vicarious thrills defy the rules that the parents have learned from their own families of origin—rules that they seemingly endorse for themselves but do not really like.

When your parents see you indulge an impulse that was forbidden to them, this helps partially satisfy these repressed urges (Slipp 1984). Therefore, they may encourage you to do what they are forbidden to do. But at the same time, they verbally deny that they want you to act this way. If you are too successful in engaging in the forbidden behavior, you cannot help but trigger their fears about not following the rules. Consequently, they may at first encourage some behavior in you but then suddenly become highly critical of it. Or they may suddenly abandon you when you are on the verge of succeeding in that endeavor. Or they may seem to get depressed about it. These *double messages* that so confuse you indicate parental ambivalence that is making the parent act in unstable ways.

The two most common CCRTs in parents that are triggered when you act out a parent's forbidden impulses involve family and cultural rules about the freedom to choose your own career path or to express your anger. Let's look at how each of these can play out.

Wilson's Story: Career Path

Carol came from a traditional family that frowned on careers for women, but she was a very ambitious, energetic, and capable woman who had always secretly dreamed of becoming a doctor. In college, however, she elected to follow the family rules and went there only to get her "MRS degree" (once a common term for a "coed's" effort to find a spouse rather than a profession), using various defense mechanisms and negative thoughts about her career abilities to justify this choice to herself.

Years later, as a parent, Carol pushed and pushed her son Wilson to become the doctor she herself secretly wanted to be. Wilson really had no interest in medicine; his true desires were for something entirely different. Nonetheless, he followed his mother's wishes and went to medical school just for her sake. When it was time for his graduation ceremony, however, she refused to come. She said she was just too depressed. Wilson had no idea how to interpret this behavior. Hadn't he done a good thing? Shouldn't his mother be happy that her wish for him had come true? So Wilson, in a bizarre compromise that is not atypical for people facing a dilemma like this, got his degree, but then kept failing to show up for his residency. That way, while Carol got some vicarious satisfaction of her ambition, Wilson didn't give her too much.

Joey's Story: Acting Out Anger

Joey kept getting in trouble at work because he would become somewhat verbally aggressive if he thought his boss was disrespecting him. Because of his mouth, Joey was in danger of losing his job. When he described his interactions with his boss to his father, Pete, his dad was outwardly critical of him but really seemed to experience glee hearing about his son's behavior. Pete couldn't suppress a smile, and there was a glint in his eye even as he told his son to be more conciliatory. He repeatedly told the story of Joey's various negative encounters with the boss to any friend who would listen.

Furthermore, he seemed to revel in lecturing Joey about the importance of keeping a job in order to support one's family. Pete repeated himself, over and over again, as if Joey had not heard him the first dozen times. Joey responded, "Do I have to listen to this?" A more appropriate comment would have been, "I heard you the first time. Stop repeating yourself!" If Joey really did not want to listen to the rants, all he needed to do was what he was being told to do. The wording of his question omitted what was, covertly, the most important issue for him. What he was actually thinking was, Do I have to keep listening to this in order to keep you happy?

Pete himself had long been stuck in a job he hated with a boss he despised. However, his Depression-era parents lived by a paradigm that if they lost a job they were not likely to find another. This impressed on Pete the importance of keeping his nose to the grindstone and putting up with whatever nonsense he had to. Watching Joey gave Pete some vicarious satisfaction of his suppressed urge to tell off his own boss. Since Pete had never spoken much about his experiences with Joey's grandparents, Joey had no way of understanding his father's confusing behavior.

Why Is Doing This Dangerous?

If you act out, say, your mother's repressed ambition, the problems you create for yourself depend somewhat on whether your inner ambition coincides with hers. In Wilson's case, it did not. He had to give up doing what he really wanted to do. However, either way, Carol's CCRT was still going to be activated as he got closer to the goal of becoming a physician. She became even more unhappy than she had been before, as his success deepened her own sense of loss. The "help" he provided to her eventually backfired, because what he was helping was Carol's avoidance of her own issues.

The downside of acting out a parent's repressed anger is clear. First, Joey was in danger of being unemployed without having arranged for another job. And again, his acting out served as a "safety valve" for Pete, but ultimately that meant Pete was continuing to avoid his issues—and was left covertly feeling guilty about how Joey's financial position might turn out.

Becoming Dependent to Prevent a Pathological Empty-Nest Syndrome

Some parents live and breathe being moms and dads, and they begin to become unstable when their children grow up and start to leave home. When they are no longer needed in the capacity of traditional family caretakers, they start to feel useless, and they develop a sort of pathological empty-nest syndrome. Plus, they begin feeling increased temptation to engage in long-repressed desires and forbidden pleasures, while remaining deathly afraid of doing so. They had probably been taught that self-indulgence was a sin that could lead to catastrophic consequences. Additionally, if their marriage was entirely based on their roles as parents and little else, once the kids are gone, long-ignored disagreements between them may surface.

Often, their forefathers and foremothers had to constantly stick together to survive, for one reason or another, and they learned early on that their whole purpose in life was to take care of their families both financially and emotionally. Alternatively, they may feel guilty about having had to both work away from home in order to make ends meet, leaving their children on their own or at daycare for extended periods. Their own parents may have been critical of them for this, repeating oft-told horror stories about the dangers of children growing up without a stay-at-home parent. In response, they may try to atone for their guilt by overindulging or overprotecting their kids, and in the process convey to their child that they need the child to remain dependent on them.

If you have parents like these, you may have remained financially or emotionally dependent on them in some way so they could continue to feel needed and have a purpose in life. You may be afraid that if you become too independent of them they will become depressed, act out, or have marital problems. In response, you may have partially failed in some aspect of your life, like work or love, necessitating your frequent return to the nest for financial or emotional support. To prevent your parents from blaming themselves for your lack of independence or from feeling as though they had been inadequate parents, you may have found a way to blame your problems on your own inadequacies or disabilities.

Allie's Story: Relationship Boomerang

Allie was unemployed and lived next door to her parents, Shanna and Ezra, in a home that they owned. She spent much of her time with them. She was on permanent disability for bipolar disorder, a severe psychiatric condition in which from time to time patients experience episodes of mania—extreme hyperactivity, poor impulse control, and impaired judgment—as well as episodes of severe depression in which they become nonfunctional. However, bipolar disorder should almost never be a cause for permanent disability. In the vast majority of cases, it is a very treatable illness. In between episodes of mania and bipolar depression, sufferers are essentially completely normal and have no trouble keeping a job. Except in severely intractable cases, medication can prevent manic episodes from ever occurring and can end depressive episodes within a few weeks.

In Allie's case, it turned out that whenever she went out and started looking for a job, she would stop taking her mood-stabilizing medication and eventually have a bipolar episode. She managed to find a psychiatrist who neglected to monitor her medication as a good doctor ought to. This doctor filled out the paperwork allowing Allie to apply for and eventually obtain Social Security disability.

In addition to spending considerable time looking after Allie without complaint, Shanna and Ezra always seemed to be inundated with requests by their other children and grandchildren to help them out financially and emotionally. At any given time, one or two of them would be living with the elderly couple, rent free. Shanna and Ezra rarely spent time together alone, and on the few occasions when they did, they usually bickered incessantly. Because they were always busy taking care of family members and spending every spare dollar

*on them, they rarely socialized with friends, never traveled or
even took vacations, and had no hobbies.*

Why Is Doing This Dangerous?

As with all dysfunctional behavior, the children sacrifice the
satisfaction and fulfillment of developing their talents and potenti-
alities. They don't get to lead their own independent lives and be all
they can be. For example, as a child, Allie had thought a lot about a
career in a field that she found fascinating, but she barely got a
chance to try it on for size. The parents in these cases never get the
satisfaction of self-actualizing either. In the long run, the adult
child's apparent neediness forces the parents to stay in their designated role. Who knows what pleasures Allie and her parents might
have been sacrificing?

Mediating Parental Discord

Children are sometimes roped into their parents' marital disputes, a
process known as "triangulation." Parents who should be in marital
counseling or even getting divorced may not believe in either one of
those options; instead, they look to their children to serve as a buffer
between them to make their lives tolerable.

Parents who do not resolve their own marital woes often have
been brought up in families or cultures in which divorce was either
frowned on or might lead to excommunication from a church. Or
they may have come from a culture that mandates that they keep
personal problems private because outsiders are not trusted, which
makes consulting a marriage counselor out of the question. This can
stem from a history of being part of a minority culture that has been
oppressed by untrustworthy outsiders, or from having been part of
an honor-based culture in which admission of problems to outsiders
will result in loss of family status.

One or both parents may use their child as a confidant to complain about the other parent. Sometimes the parent may even subconsciously induce that child to act as a sort of surrogate spouse—providing to that parent what the real spouse is not providing. Such adult children have to be "on call," ready to drop all their responsibilities at a moment's notice in order to overtly and directly settle or mediate their parents' marital disputes. If you have volunteered for one of these jobs, you may have experienced the overly demanding aspect of ICDD parenting behavior. Through their perpetual need for your services, one parent or both may interfere with your pursuit of your own interests. A common complication for the child providing this service is feeling pressured to remain single, unlike their siblings. The parents in these cases often make a statement to the effect that they "do not feel right" asking married children to come over and take care of things, because "They have their own families."

Janis's Story: Standing Up to Men

Janis was continuously "on call" for her mother, Jessica, and always went over to her parents' home whenever Jessica asked. Jessica was constantly asking Janis to run interference in the mother's relationship with Janis's father. Jessica was subservient to her husband, and she was also not supposed to be able to fix things around the house because that was designated "a man's job." The father would nonetheless often procrastinate about household tasks that needed doing—probably because of his own ambivalence over his traditional male gender role—yet would get upset if Jessica called an outside repairman to take care of it. Jessica would then go to her daughter and say, "Go tell your father to do such and such; he won't do it if I ask him, but he will for you."

Janis worked in a professional firm. She limited her own dating to men who only wanted to be "friends with benefits," so she never seemed to be able to achieve any sort of successful long-term relationship. She did this precisely because she had to be available for her mother; her trysts were a kind of compromise that allowed her to enjoy sex and some minor relationship satisfaction while continuing to stabilize her mother.

Janis actually had a second job helping to stabilize her mother: she was acting out her mom's repressed anger at men (especially at Janis's father for not keeping up his part of the bargain regarding his household duties). Jessica seemed to be critical of Janis because the daughter was highly assertive, if not aggressive, with the male superiors with whom she worked. Jessica, of course, could not be assertive with her own husband.

Jessica was vicariously expressing her anger through Janis. Interestingly, Jessica would say to Janis, "I can't believe you talk to these men that way!" Of course this sounded like a criticism, and she said it in a critical tone. However, unlike the statement, "You shouldn't talk to such men that way!" the words in her statement actually contained no value judgment at all. In fact, the mother could—and I believe actually did—admire her daughter for being willing and able to stand up to males. In fact, Jessica counted on Janis to stand up to her own husband on her behalf.

Why Is Doing This Dangerous?

The biggest problem for your personal life here is that you have to be "on call" for your parents and do not have the time to devote to other aspects of your own life such as your relationships or career. You may need to live near the folks and act like a pseudo-spouse to your parents. The parents in this situation also suffer in the long run, because your behavior allows them to stay in an unhappy marriage without ever either repairing it or leaving it.

Helping with Parental Dependency Conflicts

This problem occurs in families with legacies similar to the one described in Wilson's story. A bright, energetic, and secretly ambitious woman is taught as a child to be dependent on men and to defer to men in most major decisions. So she subconsciously chooses to marry a man who is inadequate in some way. While appearing to follow the family mandate, she is "forced" to be in charge of a lot of things by his abdication of the traditional male role, which allows her to indulge her own hidden desires to do just that. She may describe her man as being "never there for me." He may be a poor provider, generally unwilling to work hard, or a serial philanderer, or he may act like a hound dog snooping round her door (apologies to Leiber and Stoller). He may even desert the family altogether.

This kind of mother then turns to a son to be the "man of the house" to replace the absent father. If you are such a son, when you get older, you may be on call to make household repairs and the like. Your job is to do all the things that men, but not women, are supposed to be able to do. Your mother builds your ego by telling you how great you are, but she nonetheless complains that the things you do to help her are never done quite right. She secretly resents you for even thinking she cannot take care of these things herself, even though she frequently proclaims how helpless she is. In reality she is not—nor does she really want to be—as dependent as she may appear. The more you try to meet her needs, the more she seems dissatisfied. She acts like what therapists used to call a "help-rejecting complainer."

Leon's Story: Meeting Unending Demands

Leon was annoyed with his mother, Gracie, because she constantly asked him to take care of chores around her house that she was clearly capable of performing herself. He had complained to her that he was busy with a thousand things at his own job, but she just ignored his protestations and continued to lay guilt trips on him if he would not come over and take care of her requests whenever she desired. She even made her demands at times that she should have known were inconvenient for him. Furthermore, no matter how well he did a job for her, she would always find fault with it and then ask him to take even more time correcting the "problems" he could barely even perceive. And yet, he kept coming when she called.

Gracie's mother was a traditional woman who had emphasized the idea that women should not be expected to perform household repairs. Gracie was the oldest of three girls, and her father always acted like he was disappointed that she had not been born a boy. He expected her to accompany him on activities traditionally pursued by fathers and sons; he even had a nickname for her that was a boy's name. Not surprisingly, Gracie had conflicts over being dependent on males.

Why Is Doing This Dangerous?

People who do the job of helpmate (or companion) must act like they are confident, but the constant criticisms from the parent saddles them with feelings of inadequacy. They are also chronically angry, particularly at parents of the opposite sex if the job is entangled with society's gender roles. That serves no one well. And the job of a helpmate who at first is idealized and then is denigrated and criticized as inadequate does nothing to solve the parent's problem in the long run.

Letting Your Parents Run Your Life: Managing Parental Guilt

The media in modern Western culture showcase both men and women who seem to be successful in "having it all"—a satisfying career, successful marriage, happy and well-adjusted children, the works—as if they have worked out all the logistics. The fact remains that they have not; managing life on all these fronts at once is still a struggle for almost everyone except those with a large stack of inherited wealth.

On the other hand, the media is also rife with studies showing that "latchkey" children and children left in day care because both parents are working outside the home do not turn out as well, on average, as children with at least one stay-at-home parent. Today's parents are bombarded with these conflicting messages, and worry that their career aspirations or love for their jobs are short-changing their kids. The grandparents may also be critical of them for the limited amount of time they can spend with their children, thereby putting old and maladaptive family rules into play.

In response to this guilt and pressure, today's parents are susceptible to becoming closely enmeshed with their children, overindulging and overprotecting them, trying to run their lives—functioning as what are now called "helicopter parents." Even when the children have grown, the parents seem to constantly monitor their every move. The children pick up on their parents' constant guilt and feel motivated to try to make the parents more stable. If you are in this situation, your parents' hyperconcern over your ability to take good care of yourself is deeply invalidating. Do they think you are inadequate or a complete moron? This dynamic is a prime example of the issues behind invalidating and intrusive behavior from a parent. Parental hyperconcern and intrusiveness can have other, more complex causes, but the effect is the same. Getting to a root cause is nonetheless very important when it comes to putting a stop to the pattern.

When your parent seems so desperate to give you everything you need and to protect you from all harm, you may well, in the interests of stabilizing them, just give in and allow them to continue. So you might be putting up with their constant intrusiveness, pushiness, and advice—all the while swallowing your rage at them for their constant interference and insulting attitude.

Do note that in cases somewhat like this, in which the parent's guilt is mixed with a great deal of anger at the children, and the parent oscillates between hostile overinvolvement and hostile underinvolvement with an adult child, the child may develop borderline personality disorder. This serious condition is characterized by extreme emotional instability, self-injurious behavior, anger, identity confusion, and impulsiveness. For adult children in this situation, following any of the recommendations in this book absolutely requires the assistance of a knowledgeable therapist.

Let's look at several examples of parental overcontrol and intrusiveness extending well beyond childhood.

Brett's Story: Guilted into Incompetence

Brett described himself as a "nebbish," a passive, timid sort who allowed friends, coworkers, and romantic partners to take advantage of his good nature and use him in a variety of ways. He would never speak up for himself or call people out for abusing his time and generosity.

His mother, Vivian, seemed obsessed with his behavior in this regard. She called him on the phone two or three times a day to check up on him, offering a steady stream of completely obvious advice about how he could be more assertive. He always listened intently, but somehow he never seemed to learn anything. At times, Vivian would even find the phone numbers of other adults whom she believed were misusing her son and call to scold them. When Brett was in college, more than once she had gone to his professors to complain that her son had been graded unfairly.

Maya's Story: The Threat of Independence

Maya, a married mother of a teenager, had severe anxiety and sadness that led to her dropping out of a graduate degree program. The decision to leave school and return to her hometown was precipitated by daily phone calls from her mother, Autumn, in which she compulsively inquired about Maya's mental health as she tried to negotiate going to school and taking care of her teenager.

Maya did not want to blame her mother for her decision to drop out, so she came up with two rationalizations for her behavior. She first told herself that she actually wanted to drop out. Second, she blamed her husband, Bill. He had kept criticizing the program she was in, urging her to quit, and then had spent all the money she would need for another program on something else. In the husband's defense, as it turned out, Maya had complained to him about the program for years; she had never said anything good about it. And she had urged him to spend that money.

The true cause for Maya's negative view of the program was her mother's prodding. The whole time Maya was in graduate school, her mother had called her every day, expressing concern about how Maya was holding up trying to take care of Bill and their child while going to school. "How are you managing to cook for the family?" her mother would ask. "Isn't this all too much?" Maya had finally had enough and eased her mother's multiple concerns by dropping out.

Interestingly, each of Maya's parents had entered a graduate program but did not complete it. When her father was about to get his degree, the close-knit community from which they came offered him a job he felt he could not refuse. Autumn had stopped short of getting the advanced degree that she had been pursuing because she felt guilty that she was depending on the then-teenaged Maya to entertain at the family's frequent social gatherings.

The family's conflicts were shared by the larger ethnic group to which they belonged, a fundamentalist religious group that had splintered off from a larger Midwestern group and migrated west. The split in the group was, theologically speaking, about how independent group members should be allowed to be. And the breakup of the formerly monolithic group had been quite traumatic to all involved.

Autumn's excessive concern and ambivalence about how Maya was faring while away at school was almost identical to the ambivalence about the group's move west, which was reflected in group behavior within Maya's community. People leaving the group to go off to college were highly admired, even envied, but would then be pressured to return to the community with comments such as, "I don't know how you can leave the security of our community and work in those scary big cities."

Maya's case is a great example of how a mother's ambivalence, based on a larger cultural conflict, can reinforce similar conflicts in a daughter, which in turn can lead her to self-sacrificial behavior to maintain the family homeostasis. In this case, had Maya gotten her advanced degree, several problems might have ensued: Maya's success might have increased her father's depression over his own thwarted ambitions, and her mother could have been reminded of all that she had missed out on and might have blamed her husband; Maya's success would have created discord in her parents' marriage.

Why Is Doing This Dangerous?

Of course, Maya got even more anxious when she quit school, for two reasons: she was not getting to follow her dreams, and the problem with her parents still was not solved. Now they were all worried about how she was coping with her decision to quit school. There was no way for her *not* to remind her parents of their own ambivalence—and there's the rub. Whatever decision you make on how to behave vis-à-vis the focus of your family's CCRT, it will remind them of one side of their internal conflict or the other.

EXERCISE: What Interactions with Your Parents Do You Want to Change?

Review what you have written in your journal so far, then list the specific repetitive parental behavior you want them to stop. Think about how you have had to mold yourself in response so as to stabilize your parents, then write down your answers to the following questions. Since there are a number of ways that any particular pattern can play out in a given family, be as specific as possible about what you want a parent to stop *doing* or *saying*.

- What are the repetitive patterns?

- What CCRT are you helping them deal with?

- What unfulfilled need of theirs might you be taking care of?

- What might you be helping your parents avoid?

- How have your parents continued to fuel the behavior that you no longer want to engage in?

You can also begin to think about what you would want your life to be like when you no longer need to worry about stabilizing your parents or being at their mercy. You may have been so busy playing your role that you have not thought much about what you really want out of your life. The prospect of doing so may turn out to be unnerving and even depressing (we'll discuss this further in the Conclusion), so do not feel at this point that you must be able to come up with anything definitive. You'll get another chance to do this exercise later.

Thinking about all your parents' behaviors and your frustrations has probably been rather painful, but the vast majority of people have strength enough to weather it, with the prospect of addressing and relieving that pain. And you are more likely to successfully make changes when you are clear about how the problem is playing out. In the next chapter, you will learn how to investigate the history behind your parents' ICDD behavior and the origins and manifestations of family rules over at least three generations.

Learning the *reasons* for the development of their internal conflicts, as well as *how* they developed them, will allow you to be more understanding of your parents' behavior—without agreeing that it is okay for them to act the way they do. This understanding is absolutely essential to helping you to get past your own automatic responses to them and effectively make use of the various strategies and countermoves to parental invalidation that will help you put a stop to problematic interactions, free you to further self-actualize, and perhaps even achieve some form of satisfying and lasting intimacy with your parents.

CHAPTER 3

Gain Perspective by Considering Family History and Circumstances

In this chapter, you will learn how to obtain and interpret your family history in order to explain how and why your parents (or parental figures) developed specific CCRTs. Again, CCRTs are internal conflicts that a family shares over how different members are supposed to behave and the roles they are supposed to play in various social contexts. CCRTs create conflicts for your parents over previously established family rules and lead to their ICDD interactions with you. Later in the book, you'll learn how to use the family history you obtain to help you design effective interventions to resolve ongoing dysfunction.

It is important to note that you will not be able to start interviewing family members to get relevant history, let alone start to resolve dysfunctional interactions, until you learn various strategies to prevent family members from responding to you with the reactions *fight* (arguing or defending), *flight* (avoiding you as much as possible), or *freeze* (refusing to discuss important topics). While most people tend to procrastinate when it comes to starting this interview process, some jump in too quickly. This is one reason why I strongly advise you to finish reading the rest of this book in its entirety *before* proceeding to follow any of its advice. Please be patient; as you absorb the rest of the book, the logic behind this caution will become clear.

Your Parents' Histories

The issues you have identified as CCRTs for your parents can suggest questions you should ask as you look into your parents' historical family and cultural background that may have led to their problematic behavior. In this section, we will discuss how you can do some research on the rules under which your parents and grandparents grew up. As you will see, your parent's upbringing and your family's past affected the roles they play and the intrapsychic conflicts they developed.

I find that writing out your family history or *genogram* (an outline of the family's experiences and behavior patterns over several generations) in narrative form is more useful than the typical family tree diagram seen in genealogical records and television shows such as *Who Do You Think You Are?* or *Finding Your Roots.* The narrative you construct needs to be focused primarily on your parents' upbringing and their relationship with your grandparents, as well as important events in their lives (particularly as children and young adults) that may have created intrapsychic conflicts. If possible, you might also include important information about your great-grandparents' living situation and the childhoods of your grandparents.

You may already have heard stories from your parents about their childhood and about your grandparents. Such stories can often be quite revealing, because people naturally tend to talk about their most memorable interactions. What may make them memorable is that they are prototypical—they are pithy and brilliantly illustrative examples of emotionally significant interactions that recurred many times and are emblematic of the family's CCRTs. For example, Wilson, whom we met in the last chapter, was pressured to become a doctor by his mother. He learned that the role of women and their repressed ambitions were paramount for his mother. She had told stories about growing up in a fundamentalist church that preached that women should be subservient. She talked about how her parents gave her a hard time for even thinking of going to college, but none-theless spoke proudly of her defiance when she decided to go anyway. Her holiday memories during that time were all about their pressure as they introduced her to various potential suitors. She grinned as she told Wilson about her response: she would yell at her mother, "If you like him so much, *you* marry him!"

Another example of a revealing prototypical story comes from Daniel, a man from a Jewish family that seemed to value being as inconspicuous as possible. His parents would strongly discourage any behavior that even suggested showing off or becoming the center of attention. When thinking about this, he remembered hearing a story from his grandfather about being in his own parents' tavern in Czarist Russia during a pogrom, when a group of Cossacks paraded through town carrying the head of a Jew they had killed. The parade stopped in front of their tavern, and several of the men came in for a drink. Better to not stand out much in that kind of environment!

You may also need to include in your narrative description other first-degree relatives. In many cultures, your "job" or role in the family is determined by birth order, although sometimes a family will rebel against their cultural norms and reverse the jobs that would normally be assigned to oldest, middle, and youngest children. (I will discuss this in more detail later in this chapter, and again in chapter 7, Bring Significant Others and Siblings on Board.) Also, one sibling may act out one side of a parent figure's CCRT in a polarized fashion, while another sibling acts out the other side with equal polarization. A father conflicted over hard work may have one son who is a workaholic like him and another son who is a complete slacker who refuses to work at all. And your parents may no longer be performing a service that was once theirs to do, because a sibling has stepped in and relieved them of it ("sibling substitution"), but their ambivalence over that job remains. Issues involving other close relatives are yet more clues to help you understand the nature of your parents' CCRTs.

EXERCISE: Gather the Stories You Know

Write down the stories you have heard from your parents and your first-degree relatives about their pasts. Leave room in your narrative to later add descriptors of their character traits, important relationships, and relevant environmental events as you learn more and more.

Sources for Learning More

When it comes to identifying shared conflicts in families, *details matter*. Genograms should eventually include information about both the specific subject matter over which the family interacts in problematic ways and the usual ways they interact over those issues. Also keep in mind that, for example, a father and son can simultaneously have a positive and close relationship over some matters, like their jobs, while having a distant and hostile relationship when it comes to other matters, such as their religion.

People have recently begun to flock to genealogy libraries and websites like Ancestry.com to research birth and marriage records, census data, logs of ships that transported their ancestors from one country to another, and other sources of vital statistics about members of their extended families. These sources usually contain the names of our forebears and their immediate families and what they may have done for a living, as well as the years and places of their births, marriages, and deaths, and records of their migrations from country to country. While these sources of information can indeed be helpful in getting hints about problems and conflicts within a given family, they rarely give any detail about the personalities of the people involved or what their relationship patterns may have been like, or family attitudes toward things such as gender roles or class. Therefore, their usefulness is somewhat limited.

Your Parents

Your parents are the first stop on your research journey. After completing your reading of the rest of this book, you will start by asking them questions directly. If they ask why you want to know about their background, just say you have developed an interest in your family's genealogy or that you would like to get to know them better. Do not at first allude to the interactions with them that you are trying to understand unless they press you about why certain information is important to you, or seem suspicious about what you intend to do with the information, or even ask you directly whether your curiosity has anything to do with any of their behavior that you may have complained about in the past. In that case, be honest: go ahead and admit that you hope the information will help all of you get along better. Be as brief as you can.

If you find that your parents strongly resist even minimal efforts on your part to learn about their backgrounds, or if they start attacking you for even asking, you will need to back off and instead use the metacommunication skills you will learn in later chapters to get past their resistance to telling you about their backgrounds. When you've made some progress with these, you can try again to elicit genogram details.

When you ask your parents about their family background, they may also recall prototypical interactions between key family members, and you can use these as jumping-off points for further questioning about potential family issues. New information may emerge later, at any time during any of the tasks described in this book, such as while interviewing other relatives or even during metacommunication with your parents over ICDD behavior. Any such information will suggest even more questions you can ask to further clarify your family dynamics.

To reduce the likelihood of overly emotional responses, spread your questioning over several shorter interviews. Begin by asking your parents for more information and details about their childhoods—particularly about their relationships with each of their own parents. Start with nonthreatening questions like names and occupations of important relatives, whom they were closest to in the family, or what was going on in their neighborhoods when they were growing up. Early on, open-ended questions are best, such as "What was it like for you growing up?" and "What was Grandma like when you were a teenager?" Ask about their experiences in school and in their early careers. How old were they when they left home? Important questions include how your parents met, and whether both sets of grandparents were happy or upset about their union.

If you do not encounter much resistance to discussing family history as you proceed, gradually move into potentially more threatening areas such as those discussed later in this chapter. Try to discreetly zero in on family problems. Was the marriage between your grandparents their first marriage? What do your parents know about any prior or subsequent grandparental marriages? If their parents were divorced, ask them if they know why their parents split. Which parent did they then stay with? Was the noncustodial parent involved in their life or pay child support?

Even if a parent begins to open up, early on, you should avoid asking for too many details about aspects of their childhood that seem to cause them discomfort, or about which they have always been rather touchy. If you suspect a family history of physical or sexual abuse, severe substance abuse, criminal activities, or domestic violence, your questions about times when those issues were at play may touch on family secrets and skeletons in the family closet that your parents will be loath to reveal, because of both their shame and family rules against discussing these things. Later on, when you are attempting to metacommunicate specifically about the ICDD interactions, you can use the skills described in the rest of the book to obtain even more information as the process unfolds. At that point, you can and should, in most cases, press for details about family secrets. But not yet. Save those efforts for the metacommunication stage.

Other Older Relatives

Regardless of whether your parents seem reluctant to discuss certain parts of their past histories, sometimes an aunt or uncle may be more open about their experiences as children. Many families have one person who serves as a sort of family historian and who may even be aware of some relevant events and characteristics of important family members about which your parents are unaware. Think about who in your extended family is the most open; go to that family member and follow the same strategies recommended for interviewing your parents. Again, write down everything as soon as possible afterward.

If your grandparents are still alive, they are definitely worth interviewing, again using the same strategies. They are the ones most likely to know about your great-grandparents or even your great-great-grandparents (their own grandparents) if the problematic behavior seems to go back that many generations. Of course, you will not necessarily know how far back they go unless you start asking questions. Some family members are open and can tell you a lot, whereas others are secretive and less revealing. Getting information from relatives who fall into the latter category can be quite challenging. For highly secretive families, a knowledgeable therapist might be better at helping you get it out of them than a book like this one.

You may have some concerns that these relatives will go to your parents and tell them you were inquiring about forbidden subjects. If so, you can use the detriangulation strategies described in chapter 7 to minimize any potential damage.

Clearly, the older you are, the fewer family resources will be available. This is why you should, if at all possible, interview grandparents, great-aunts and -uncles, and older cousins while they are alive and in control of their faculties. Do not procrastinate; deaths can happen or dementia arise quite unexpectedly. If all of them are deceased or the living have memory issues, you may have to make guesses about the development of CCRTs based on whatever information you already have about your parents' upbringing.

When the ICDD patterns go back to a fourth or even a fifth generation, there is seldom a trail available to follow other than traditional genealogical sources. However, you can usually come up with an educated guess about what may have happened that created conflicts within and between members of the extended family.

I suggest you focus on several factors affecting families that are often central to uncovering the rules and norms that shape your parents' and parental figures' ICDD behavior; these factors will be discussed in the sections that follow. Your goal is to generate hypotheses about the origins of your parents' conflicts. You can use these as the basis for formulating a strategy to get past their formidable defenses. Then you will be able to work on changing dysfunctional patterns with a high degree of relevance to your own dysfunctional family dynamics. Consider how the following topics relate to your family history, and include them as you interview family members.

Ethnic Norms: Your Culture and Subculture

Different ethnic groups have different rules of behavior and customs in work, marriage, childrearing, and the like, so it can be very useful to know about the typical rules and customs of your parents' and grandparents' cultural groups. They can help you identify which of these have created conflicts when they become problematic due to cultural changes and historical events. The best source for learning even more about family norms in your own culture and subculture is the book *Ethnicity and Family Therapy* (McGoldrick, Pearce, and Giordano 2005).

Before discussing this further, I want to address the elephant in the room. Whenever anyone deals with subjects like these, they are in danger of feeding into, being criticized for discussing, or even helping to create cultural stereotypes that can easily become caricatures. To avoid this pitfall, keep in mind that many members of any ethnic group do not conform to even relatively authentic cultural norms that arise from the historical experiences of their group. The members of different ethnic groups, although they often (but not always) have certain commonalities, are nonetheless quite diverse. To determine the extent to which particular families do or do not fit into a traditional paradigm, consider whether they lived in an ethnic neighborhood; their upward mobility and socioeconomic status, educational achievement, and prevalence of intermarriage; and the strength of their political and religious ties to their group. All of these variables create a variety of experiences.

Immigration Dynamics

The timing of immigration to other countries and the reception that immigrants received from their new country are also major factors shaping their attitudes about their own cultural norms. Depending to some extent on the reason for the move, immigration often leads to situations in which children seem to have one foot in their culture of origin and the other in their new culture. Kids originally from traditional societies, for example, may go to school right alongside their more individualistic Western schoolmates and try to fit in, but their resulting behavior may upset their parents, who see it as decadent and disrespectful. Conflict is set up when, in different social contexts, the children of immigrants are placed in situations in which they must follow one or the other of two conflicting sets of rules. Whatever rules they originally grew up with that put them into the situation become CCRTs for them.

This is also true, to a lesser extent, for their parents. Nonetheless, the conflict as it is expressed in their parents may be just as toxic. These parents often do not have the same level of contact with the outside ambient culture as do their children. Their interactions tend to take place mostly with other adults from their own ethnic group. However, their social isolation is far from complete, since they are frequently exposed to local television and other media with their depictions of typical life in that country. In America, they are exposed to the alluring invitation, exemplified in an old beer commercial, to "live with all the gusto you can." But they tend to feel far less free to accept it than their children do.

At the same time, given their children's language skills and familiarity with the environment in which the family now resides, the parents may become dependent on their children to help them interact with the larger culture when the need arises. This often sets up a situation in which the parents seem to push their progeny to become acculturated—yet loudly object if they do so. The potential for double messages and the creation of ongoing dysfunctional behavior patterns becomes very significant.

Interestingly, reversals of this pattern may also be found. According to one study of Mexican-American families (Lau et al. 2005), there were instances when a member of the younger generation was *more* aligned with the traditional culture than the parents were. This created even more problems than when the opposite was the case. Some families and family members rebel *against* their original cultural norms and go to opposite extremes to disprove stereotypes. This tendency often divides members of a particular group into two subgroups that seem to be polar opposites of one another on any given dimension. Recall our earlier discussion of polarized behavior. For another example, African-American psychologist Nancy Boyd-Franklin (1989) discusses how the experiences of Blacks in slave times has led to a cultural legacy in which some African-American families tend to treat their lighter-skinned members better than the darker-skinned ones. However, other families have reacted strongly against this and tend to favor their darker-skinned members, as dramatized in Spike Lee's 1998 movie *School Daze*.

As you construct your genogram, ask these key questions: When and under what circumstance did your forebears immigrate? How long has your family been in the country in which you reside? How different was the culture they came from, and in what ways? Were they part of a culture that was widely discriminated against in the new country?

Silenced Sources of Shame

A caution here: some important patterns may be hard to discern. Some issues, although common and impactful, may have been kept hidden because of widespread feelings of shame. In her fascinating book *Family Secrets: Shame and Privacy in Modern Britain* (2013), Deborah Cohen discusses an interesting example of this in Britain. I want to share it because her descriptions provide an excellent illustration of how historical developments can greatly impact family dynamics for generations to come.

The British occupation of India in the nineteenth and twentieth centuries led some men to be separated from their wives for extended periods. These wives often had paramours. If they became pregnant, they often wanted to adopt out the baby to hide it from their husbands. England had exceedingly harsh laws about children who were born out of wedlock, intended to inflict the sins of the parents upon these children. Because of societal attitudes such as these, often adopted children were never told they were adopted. Adoptive parents, anxious to prevent the child's learning the truth, wanted as few people as possible to know about the adoption; they even kept the secret from the child's adoptive siblings. Birth certificates were routinely altered. But the adopted children still might have figured out they were adopted, based on clues such as their physical appearance or on overheard conversations.

This fear of discovery understandably had a negative effect on the relationships between many adopted children and their parents. This in turn may have led adopted children to develop any number of problematic attitudes, which later on might affect their relationships with their own children. For example, adopted children who had not figured out that they were adopted might have thought that the parents were ashamed of them, creating a self-fulfilling prophecy that they would become failures in life.

The presence of a hidden historical issue such as this, which your parents may be reacting to without even knowing why, is often indicated by what I call "plot holes." Your parents may describe somewhat extreme behavior in their own family of origin that seems to come out of nowhere and also seems grossly inconsistent with other things the various family members do and say. Your parents may offer explanations for it that do not really explain anything. In such situations, information from traditional genealogical sources like census data may offer clues as to what might have happened that led to the behavior in question.

Gender Norms

As we have already seen, one norm that has created many problematic, diverse, and widespread CCRTs is that of gender roles. Gender role norms affect a wide variety of family behaviors, including parenting, careers, sexuality, and dependency. Certainly, the emancipation of women, the continuing movement toward gender equality, and the sexual revolution are some of the greatest and most positive developments of modern times. However, because of the rapidity with which these have developed, many have had a difficult adjustment to make.

For both men and women, this change has created conflicts, confusion, and guilt matters over the issue of childcare when both parents have other work responsibilities. Conflict regarding the expected role of parents in their children's lives is perhaps *the* hot-button issue for *either* disengaged or enmeshed and overinvolved parents.

Levels of Individuation

Another major source of widespread and wide-ranging intrapsychic conflict is changing attitudes toward the individual pursuit of pleasures such as the proverbial sex, drugs, and rock and roll. Attitudes about the propriety of, say, sexual pleasure—particularly for women—have changed frequently and drastically. Those who give lip service to such issues as abstinence or reserving sex for procreation only may act in a highly hypocritical fashion in their own lives.

One surprisingly common result of shared family conflicts over such matters is the phenomenon of the family "black sheep." One family member—perhaps your parent—opts to be the rule breaker, enjoying that which is attractive—but forbidden—to all the others. While black sheep may seem to enjoy the fruits of self-indulgence—which may vicariously satisfy the hidden cravings of the rest of the family—unfortunately, that is not the only effect of their chosen way of life.

If black sheep indulge themselves and, in the process, live a successful and exciting life, they in effect disprove the family rule against engaging in whatever behavior fits the black sheep bill. When the others see this, they might start to feel regret for all they have missed out on, and ashamed of themselves for not having questioned the family rules. The black sheep, being still aware of the rules he has flouted, may feel he must demonstrate the folly of his engaging in the conflictual behavior. He may do so by creating a bad outcome, either consciously or unconsciously. He may fail in some way; for example, he may develop an addiction, contract a sexually transmitted disease, have an affair and destroy his marriage and his relationships with his children, have multiple divorces, or become a deadbeat dad. In doing so, his example is held up by the rest of the family as proof that the forbidden impulses are forbidden for good reason, and that the old family rules simply must continue to be followed. Not surprisingly, black sheep have problematic interactions with their own children. Look for evidence of black sheep behavior in family members as you construct your genogram.

Insiders and Outsiders

Another area of ethnic norms, discussed by McGoldrick et al. in *Ethnicity and Family Therapy*, is the importance of the rules governing the family's relationships with outsiders, both within and outside of their own peer group, when trouble arises. I advise looking into the following questions as they apply to your own ethnic group:

- What do families generally define as a problem?

- What do they generally see as a solution to their problems?

- To whom do they usually turn for help? Alternatively, do they hide all of their problems from their neighbors?

These rules can become the focus of double messages to you and conflicting demands made on you about relationships with people outside of the immediate family or with other ethnic groups. This was illustrated in a dramatic case of a physician from India who came to the United States to do her specialty training. She fell in love with a colleague who was of British background—the nationality of her home country's former colonial masters. Her parents in India had already arranged a marriage for her in keeping with their culture's mandates; they told her in no uncertain terms that if she defied them and married the man she loved, they would completely disown her and never speak to her again. Tragically, her dilemma led to her suicide.

Family members may also try to keep their problems from the prying eyes of any outsiders—such as a therapist—to follow the traditions of their honor-bound society, such as those found in the Middle East, or because of mistrust of the majority white culture due to past injustices. At the same time, they may be watching TV programs such as *Dr. Phil* extolling the benefits of psychotherapy. Thus a child from such a family might perceive mixed messages about seeking outside help. Another common source of ambivalence is a liberal family's concerns about hatred and animosity from their own or from the majority culture should one of their children enter a mixed-race or gay marriage.

Your Family's Constellation

The birth order and number of children, particularly in your parents' and grandparents' families of origin, often suggest some of the possible family rules and problems described in this book. In many traditional cultures, the oldest daughter's role is to function as the mother's assistant in taking care of the domicile and the other siblings, and the oldest son is expected to be the one who inherits and takes over the family business after his father passes away. Younger siblings tend to be allowed a bit more leeway; they may have the freedom to choose to do other things besides follow in their parents' footsteps, and they often are the more rebellious family members. This can lead the older sibs to be jealous of the younger ones. Conversely, the younger ones may be angry about the older sibling's status as a favored heir. In rebellious families, the duties and benefits of these sibling positions may be reversed, but not really abandoned. Families from traditional cultures often assign duties and responsibilities to their children according to both their position in the birth order and their gender.

Birth order might lead to an intrapsychic conflict in your parent. I'll discuss one scenario to illustrate how it can have cascading effects through the family and down through generations. Say the family is very large and a parent becomes ill; the presence of many children can quickly go from a being a source of joy to being hugely burdensome, with varying effects on the relationships between each child and each parent, as well as on the relationships between the parents and between the siblings. These effects can be magnified when the children grow up and have children of their own—children just like you. It may create a situation in which your parent may feel compelled to run your life, but at the same time resent the task. As a result, your mom or dad may be overbearing and controlling most of the time, and yet disappear when you need them the most.

A parent who was the oldest sibling in a large family may have had to take care of the younger children because the parents became incapacitated or neglected their parental duties. Parental neglect in a large family of children may stem from parental depression, financial pressures, substance abuse, feelings of being inadequate as a parent, or black sheep behavior such as infidelity. Sometimes it occurs in families in which a child dies from an accident or illness, and parents, in their grief, have difficulty getting close to their remaining children. In these cases, the oldest child may be ill equipped to take over as a parent, simply lacking the power and know-how to do so effectively. And when they have children of their own, they may continue to feel inadequate. In response, they may become distant and neglectful of their children.

If the siblings are really angry at the neglectful parents, they may nevertheless also want to protect their parents from their own negative and dangerous feelings. They may do so by displacing (shifting) their angry feelings onto the older, parent-substitute sibling. Displacement is often thought of as a way people protect *themselves* from feelings that they find unacceptable, but this is a case of someone protecting her *parents* from feeling bad about becoming neglectful.

Early on, the caretaking sibling, because of his limitations, may inadvertently feed into the anger of siblings by taking care of them in hostile or overly controlling ways. After a time, the caretaker may subconsciously start to act even worse in this regard. This protects the parents from the siblings' anger by giving the siblings justification for focusing it on the caretaker rather than on the neglectful parents. When caretaking siblings grow up and have their own children—maybe you are one of them—they may feel the need to continue to serve the function of letting others displace anger onto them. They may act in ways that lead *you* to be angry with them as well.

This situation is a setup for disturbed sibling relationships not only during childhood, but also in their adult lives. Your aunts and uncles may exclude your parent from family gatherings or try to disinherit him when the grandparents pass away. As proxies for their parents, your parents' children—perhaps you—are often shunned as well. Alternatively, people from such families may be prone to giving one another the "silent treatment" when upset with one another, or may cut off contact with one another for years at a time. Vicious gossip about the eldest and his children may make the family rounds.

This can lead your parents, in an effort to protect you, to try to interfere when you want to reconnect with your extended family—without telling you why they object. It may appear that they think there is something wrong with *you* because you want that. Or they may think that siblings are nothing but trouble, and therefore create problems for you and your brothers and sisters by gossiping about each one of you, behind that child's back, to all the others.

This is just one scenario that can unfold in a multitude of ways. As you do your research, explore how birth order and relationships with siblings have played out.

Family Trauma and Chaos

Significant traumatic events often have long-lasting negative effects on families because they generate fear of behaving in certain ways within certain contexts. Some of these behaviors may have been highly valued before the trauma, and giving them up may have been difficult and created mixed feelings. Others, such as experiences with violence toward minorities attempting to advance socially, produce fears that are then passed down to children as the parents react negatively to aspects of their child's behavior in those contexts. The original source of the fears, however, may be completely unknown to the subsequent generations, making the parents' reactions seem crazy. This, in turn, creates confusion for the children about the reasons for family rules. Therefore, as you construct your genogram, you should always include the *timing* and *nature* of all of the following family traumas.

Illness and Death

The onset of disabilities, abdication of parental or breadwinning roles created by chronic physical illnesses or mental illnesses such as bipolar disorder or substance abuse, or an early parent death—all of these create trauma and chaos. Under these conditions, the presence of children can suddenly change from being a joy to being a major burden, with the parents feeling guilty about feeling like this. We have seen how this might affect sibling relationships among the children. Alternatively, children may, in an effort to unburden their parents, leave home before they are ready to be on their own by getting into ill-advised relationships. Continuing the problematic behavior into the next generation, if that relationship produces a child, the young parents may soon see that child as an impediment to leaving a problematic relationship. Alternatively, if a parent still believes that her very existence is a toxic burden on everyone, including her own children, the parent may start to avoid the children or distance from them by behaving in hateful ways.

Cheating on Spouses and Multiple Sexual Affairs

Infidelity often places children in the middle of a problem marriage. Sometimes the aggrieved party tries to alienate a child from the other parent. Other times, the aggrieved party engages in self-blame; children may try to ease that parent's self-loathing by claiming that the missing parent actually left because of the child himself, since he did not measure up in some way.

Domestic Violence

In cases of spousal abuse, children often become involved. For instance, a child might step in and try to prevent the abuse and end up getting injured. Or the child might become a parent herself while trying to manage the parents' relationship. Or an abused mother may confide her fears to a young son who is not capable of protecting her, leading him to develop chronic feelings of inadequacy as an adult. In the latter case, when he has children himself, he might try to make up for his feeling of inadequacy by becoming an overprotective helicopter parent. Alternatively, he might respond by not providing necessary and appropriate discipline for his children for fear he might do it wrong.

Child Physical, Sexual, or Emotional Abuse

People abused as children often blame themselves in order to go along with family demands meant to protect the interests of the abusive adults. Were they blamed for being a seducer or a slut? If so, they may start to consider themselves potentially toxic to their own offspring and avoid them. Or they may act in hateful ways toward their children to prove how awful they had been and how much they had deserved the abuse they received. If, in response to their own abuse, your parent has been physically or sexually abusive toward you (a common pattern), you should not attempt the steps recommended in this book on your own without the guidance of a knowledgeable therapist.

Long Separations Between Spouses

Whether due to military deployment, arrest and jail, job requirements, or immigration, long separations can lead to the other parent's feeling burdened and resentful of her children, and then guilty over harboring those feelings. Such separations may be related to periods of significant poverty or sudden reversals of fortune, such as extended periods of unemployment of a primary or secondary breadwinner. And men returning from the long separations of war may become distant and uninvolved with their children because of preoccupation with severe post-traumatic symptoms of flashbacks and nightmares about their combat experience.

Criminal Activity

Children may be pressured to participate in, or to avoid, the family "business." The mixed feelings produced by a sense of family loyalty in a situation like this were effectively dramatized in the *Godfather* movies. A possible example from real life is that of Rudy Giuliani. He was the first public official to effectively prosecute the infamous "Five Families" of the mafia in New York. Yet Giuliani's father had served prison time for armed robbery and had worked for a mob loan shark (Sapolsky 2017). While I cannot speak to what was going on in his family, for some families, such a scenario can set up a situation in which children feel torn between loyalties to the competing and completely opposite, polarized behavior exhibited by various factions of a family torn by ambivalence about being law-abiding citizens.

Racial Violence and Discrimination

In the play and movie *Fences* by August Wilson, a former player in the Negro baseball leagues before Jackie Robinson broke the color barrier in the majors is bitter because he had not been able to play there. These experiences lead him to forbid his son to accept a college football scholarship. The son attributes his father's behavior to jealousy rather than an attempt to protect the son from the bitter disappointment the father had experienced. Was your family subject to discrimination, harassment, or even violence? If so, why might that family in particular have become a target? Did racism prevent family members from reaching their full potential or force them to give up on specific talents and skills that brought them joy?

Political Activism and Its Aftermath

The experience of taking sides in political battles, within organizations as well as in society in general, has been extremely traumatic for some families. Union activities, for example, have led to violent reactions from the business establishment; antigovernment demonstrations may lead to imprisonment or, in some places, the need to flee a country. Such family experiences can lead to intense ambivalence and mixed messages over such activities as speaking out against injustice or even standing out in a crowd. Children from later generations may not have learned about the horrifying experiences of grandparents or other ancestors, and therefore may be completely mystified as to why their parents react to them so negatively when analogous issues arise in their lives.

Religious Fundamentalism and Its Dictates and Norms

Fundamentalist religions often set and enforce strict, rigid rules for their adherents, governing virtually every aspect of human behavior. These rules may often seem arbitrary or even capricious to those members who allow themselves to question them. Furthermore, they can readily observe people in the ambient culture enjoying various freedoms that are denied to members of the faith. Individuals in fundamentalist families are susceptible to becoming black sheep. In fact, other important family members may appear to *need* them to be black sheep in order to feel justified in continuing to follow oppressive religious family rules.

Mixed Marriages

In the section on insiders and outsiders, I mentioned how marriage between individuals from two different racial, ethnic, or religious groups, as well as gay marriage, can have frightening consequences because of acts of hatred and animosity from the culture at large. Violence and discrimination can traumatize the family and lead to conflicts and mixed messages about a wide variety of issues, such as trusting others or political activism.

Culturally Sanctioned Strategies and Parenting Fads

Conflicting cultural notions, along with conflicting but omnipresent advice from parenting experts, can drive parents crazy and make parent-child relationships conflicted and fraught with tension. Changing mores can lead to major battles between your parents and your grandparents over *you*. How your parents were raised, and your grandparents' emotional and negative reactions to the ways in which your parents raised you, can lead parents into a pattern of disengagement from you—or its opposite, enmeshment.

Today's parents may go from one extreme to the other or go overboard on a wide variety of childrearing issues. Concerning discipline, for example, so-called experts have gone from "spare the rod and spoil the child" to saying that a quick slap on the behind of a child about to dart out into traffic is child abuse. Some parents believe they "should" allow their children to express themselves freely; others believe that children should be seen and not heard. Parents may let their child have complete and unfettered access to the Internet or try to monitor their every mouse click.

In the latter case, children may mistakenly come to the conclusion that their parents will be disappointed if the child does *not* look at pornography or communicate with strangers—because the parents keep looking so hard for that. Because of this dynamic, parents' apparent fixation actually increases the chances that children will disregard the parents' verbal instructions and act out.

The norms for how involved parents should be with their children have also gone from one extreme to the other, often within the space of one or two generations. Today's parents often feel the need to protect their children from any and all of life's adversities—another cause of helicopter parenting—instead of allowing their children to experience life's adversities so they can become tough, resourceful, and independent. Or they may go to the other extreme and let their children pretty much fend for themselves.

In thinking about this issue, ask yourself if your parents and grandparents ever argued about how your parents disciplined you. Did they respond with confusion or anger about their parenting duties? For example, did they seem preoccupied and constantly worried about how you are doing, or seem to feel guilty that they haven't done more for you?

"Soft Is Weak"

I refer to this variation on the conflictual parent discipline problem as the "Boy Named Sue" syndrome. It applies to some parents who seem to be particularly hard on and overly critical of their child, especially those who seem obsessed with telling the child, in one way or another, that she is too weak. They punish kids for any behavior they perceive as "soft." If your parents continually criticize the softer, gentler aspects of your personality like this, before you ask them to simply stop it, you may find it helpful to understand that they may think they are doing you a favor.

Often these parents had a tough, hardscrabble childhood and adolescence. Their own parents may have made them feel ashamed of any weaknesses they were told they had or may have come to believe that they had. In response, they believe that they in turn must toughen up their own children by making sure that the children can stand up for themselves. In the process, they end up doing to their children the very things that had been done to them. They mistreat them.

This process, in an extreme version, was described in the lyrics to the Shel Silverstein poem "A Boy Named Sue," famously sung by Johnny Cash. The song was meant to be funny, and the story it tells is improbable. However, the general idea is a wonderful illustration of the process I am discussing. When the character in the song was a baby, his father abandoned the family, but just before leaving he named his son "Sue." Of course, from then on, the son is relentlessly teased and ridiculed by many people for having a girl's name and is constantly getting into fights because of it.

The son's anger that his life has been so difficult leads him to track down and plan to kill his father for doing this to him. He finally finds his dad, and they get into a brawl. Sue gets the upper hand and pulls a gun on his father. He is about to shoot when the father explains that, although he understands his son's anger and would not blame him for shooting, he had given the son that name because he knew he wasn't going to be around to protect the boy. The father thought he was ultimately doing his son a favor, as the name would force the son to "get tough or die."

We've now looked at many of the familial rules and patterns that may be the source of your parents' ICDD behavior. Next, we'll look at how you can use them to shape your family's genogram and start learning from it.

Developing Your Hypotheses

The more information you can gather about the relevant aspects of your family's genogram, the more easily you can identify the family rules with which your parent is struggling, the origins of the struggle, and therefore the possible reasons behind their annoying behavior, double messages, and conflicting demands. You will better understand what is behind some of the automatic responses they elicit from you—the relevant family patterns, where they came from, and what purpose they serve.

Of course, no matter how much information you are able to uncover, your ideas remain an educated guess rather than a proven fact. Your guess is what scientists call a "provisional hypothesis," which must be tested before it can be considered a likely truth—and even then it remains only a useful approximation and not the entire explanation. The test that the hypothesis must pass is obtaining confirmation from your parents as you attempt to discuss the family dynamics and your problematic interactions with them. As we've discussed, new information may come to light during metacommunication with your parents. This new information will require you to alter or revise your original hypothesis, allowing you to be even more empathic with their misbehavior. That being the case, even if you have had a great deal of difficulty uncovering your family's whole story, do not be afraid to make a guess anyway based on any limited information that suggests the possibility of any of the patterns discussed in this chapter.

EXERCISE: Understanding a Pattern

First, take out the narrative family history you started earlier with your recollections of family stories that have been passed down to you. Fill in the information you have learned about the patterns of behavior and important historical events and processes you have discovered in your research.

Next, take out your list of problematic interactions with your parents that you want to change. Pick one or two of them that seem most troubling for you, and see if you can at least partially explain your parents' difficult behavior. Which CCRT was created as a result?

If there are other problematic parental behavior patterns you would like to address, I suggest waiting until after you successfully address the most problematic one with your parents before bringing up additional ones. Once the family gets used to your efforts at metacommunication, things often (though not always) get easier and faster as you go along.

A provisional hypothesis could be something like, "My father is constantly on my case about my being too aggressive, because his grandfather's macho behavior led to his early death in a bar fight. Because of this, being outspoken or pushy became a subject of ambivalence for all of the males in the family." Write down your provisional hypothesis.

Eventually, bringing such patterns up for discussion in a constructive way will, if everything goes as planned, allow for everyone to reconsider the family rules, think about whether those rules still make sense, and start to recognize when they may be over- or under-reacting and creating unnecessary tension between you and them.

The Importance of Empathy

Making hypotheses about the nature and origins of your parents' problematic behavior in this way can lead you to see their behavior in a different light. You can think of it with empathy: the feeling that you understand their experiences and emotions, without necessarily agreeing that their resultant behavior is a good thing—and certainly not an excuse for mistreating you. Of course, to remain empathic when your parent is hurting, frustrating, or annoying you is a tall order. The natural response is to either respond in kind or run away. Thinking objectively and dispassionately about *why* they feel it necessary to treat you in unpleasant ways may go against every impulse you have. As one of my patients pointed out, remaining empathic when you are being attacked or invalidated is "counterinstinctual."

Providing them with empathy may seem unfair as well. Does this not mean you are letting your parents off the hook? Why should you have to, when they seem to have started the whole problem? Of course, as we have seen, the process really did not start with them, or even necessarily with *their* parents. Each generation has inherited problematic reaction patterns from the preceding one. Blaming and finger pointing, although emotionally satisfying, are counterproductive in the sense that they prevent your family members from constructively engaging with you in *problem solving.* Since the problems go back several generations anyway, I often tell my patients that if they have to blame someone, just go ahead and blame Adam and Eve—and stop there.

You may also find yourself asking why you should be the one to fix a messed-up relationship with your parents. They had these problems before you even existed; they should be the ones who take care of them. The answer to that question is a practical one: You are the one who picked up this book, so you are in a position to do something. They are not. What is "fair" and what is not "fair" is irrelevant.

The primary reason for using empathy is purely *strategic.* If instead of a family member you were a cop, a prosecutor, or a judge, I would not recommend offering any understanding at all, let alone empathy, to an adult who mistreats their children. Off with their heads! However, when we approach the situation as problem solvers, we should be mindful of how all of us are biologically built to be powerfully influenced by our kin group. You will need to maintain an empathic attitude to change their behavior regardless of whether you feel they deserve any empathy. As mentioned previously, you do not have to pretend everything is okay or condone in any way how your parents behave in order to try to be more understanding. Doing that would come off as horribly phony anyway! Not only that, but you are going to be letting them know in no uncertain terms that their behavior must change.

It is also true that, paradoxically, the reason you may not *want* to be empathic in many instances is that *they* do not seem to want you to be empathic. They may actually refuse to accept empathy, or make fun of you when you try to give it to them. When your parents repeatedly do things that annoy you, they have to know just what they are doing, and they are doing it on purpose. People who keep poking a hornet's nest with a stick are not really as oblivious to the consequences as they may seem to be. They are in fact literally "asking for it"—angling for a negative response. Your parents do this because they secretly feel guilty for the effects of their problematic behavior on you, and they secretly believe that they deserve to be punished for it. When you act angry, you are actually blindly *following* the dysfunctional rules of the family.

Ironically, you may also be *protecting* them. The desire to avoid making them feel bad is what I call the "protection racket." By not helping your parents take an honest look at their problems with you,

you may be trying to spare them the feelings of guilt, unease, shame, and low self-worth that their own behavior has created for them in the first place. Perhaps you feel they are too weak or impaired to face reality. This belief may be shared by several other family members, who constantly walk on eggshells around the parents to avoid upsetting them in any way.

Paradoxically, this family attitude actually backfires. If all of your intimates treat you as if you are weak, then you may very well start to believe that you *are* weak—regardless of whether you really are or not. In truth, people are not that fragile, and they often resent it when everyone else acts as if they are—even after they have started to believe it themselves. Overprotecting your parents has effects similar to overprotecting children. They may start to believe they are impaired and therefore must avoid anything stressful. Feeling weak actually ruins their chances for taking charge of their own lives and feeling good about themselves.

You have now taken a deep dive into your parents' psyches and come up with some preliminary ideas about the origins of their behavior that clarify it and make it seem far less unfathomable. With this knowledge in hand, the next step is to plan your strategy for metacommunicating about what you have learned and confronting the problematic interactions head-on in ways designed to finally put a stop to them.

You will begin by cataloging your parents' typical ways of getting you to shut up whenever you have tried to talk to them about these issues; then you will plan *countermoves* to keep the conversation on track. Since you have lived with them all your life, you probably can predict which measures they might employ with you, so you can plan an effective countermeasure and have it at the ready. This will provide you with all the tools you need to achieve the desired changes you have listed. In turn, this will help you to live more freely and chart your own course in life.

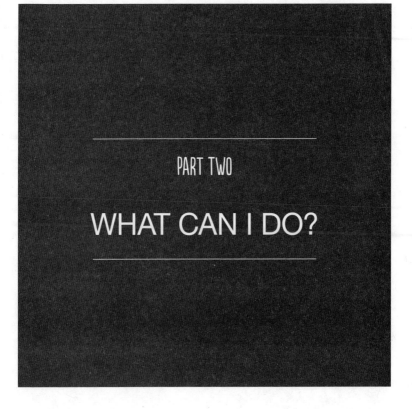

PART TWO

WHAT CAN I DO?

CHAPTER 4

Prepare Yourself

To succeed in metacommunication, after you have collected a family history and generated the relevant hypotheses, you still some have legwork and planning to do. You will need to:

- Understand and anticipate which defensive responses your parents tend to employ to mask the rules they are following and the underlying CCRT.

- Learn and plan the countermeasures you will employ to get past your parent's defenses,

- Practice using those countermeasures both firmly and empathically, via recording yourself and role-playing, so you're prepared when it comes time to begin a conversation.

Your parents and other relatives may use defensive maneuvers on you at any time to throw you off track. These are not specific to the particular goals you are trying to achieve, whether it's obtaining family history, bringing up ICDD behavior or underlying CCRTs, addressing domains of interactions, identifying particular roles your parents may be playing, or requesting specific changes. Each family member you talk to has characteristic defensive styles that may be employed at any time. Therefore, we will begin part two with some general considerations that apply to all metacommunication.

In the chapters that follow this one, we will look in detail at typical strategies people most commonly choose to block metacommunication. As I go through the various maneuvers, I will suggest the countermove for you to employ that is *most likely* to disarm your parents and push the metacommunicative process forward. Keep in mind, however, that you can modify any of my suggested defensive countermoves for use against any of the *other* defenses that I describe. What works with one family member may backfire with another, and what works best in one family may backfire in a different family—even when superficially there seems to be a lot of similarity between the two. It takes empathy to understand what, in the family member's background, might explain her defensiveness. This ability to understand will help you know how to apply the countermoves I offer in chapters 5 and 6.

First, let us examine the basics of the empathic communication that is essential to getting past your parents' defenses. You will learn how to help your parents to talk at least somewhat dispassionately about uncomfortable subjects rather than attacking you, becoming defensive, acting out, ignoring you, or employing other strategies designed to get you to back off or shut up.

Communicating Effectively Through Empathy

All people, including your parents, will invariably react negatively if they feel they are being attacked or criticized—even if they are well aware that the criticism is perfectly valid. Not only that, but if others in the family see you "attack" another family member, they will defend that person even when they themselves are also furious with him or her. Subjecting your parents to offensive accusations is the surest way to fail in solving repetitive family problems. That's why empathy is the most important tool for your successful metacommunication.

From a strategic standpoint, you should approach discussions about family dynamics as if no one involved is, deep down, a villain, no matter how awful their behavior. When you are annoyed or frustrated with someone, or righteously indignant about some behavior, this is a challenge. So here are more ways to gain a more empathic perspective on your parents.

Consider Their Underlying Motives

Remember, no matter how unreasonable your parents' behavior may seem to be, there is a reason for it and logic behind it. If you've followed the exercises in the last chapter, you have already learned a lot about the forces that have buffeted them in their lives and the motives behind what may seem to be horrid actions. As you think about their behavior and try to develop empathy for it, it's important to keep giving your parents the *benefit of the doubt* when it comes to the *motives* behind their problematic behavior. Do not automatically assume they are doing things that you do not like because they are crazy, evil, stupid, or blind. Try to think of their motives in the best possible light. You can, and certainly should, quibble with the *means* they have chosen to use in order to achieve certain ends. But try to at least respect their underlying goals to some degree.

Witness Their Powerful Fear

Another way to avoid being judgmental is to remind yourself that their invalidating, critical, or hateful responses are almost always based on their *fears* rather than on hatred or sadism. Just as you have developed protective behavior in an effort to stabilize them, their behavior has succeeded in helping stabilize their own parents. Consider, too, that in the past they may have been severely punished for admitting how they really think and feel about issues that are the subject of family ambivalence. When you bring up topics that threaten to expose these conflicts, your parents may easily start to panic. They usually will not admit that, because doing so would lead others to suspect their true, but hidden, feelings. They also may feel the need to protect third parties like Grandma by deflecting attention from underlying issues.

Be Curious About Your Own Fear

You can also develop empathy by examining your own fears about initiating the metacommunicative process described in this volume. As you think about effectively and empathically confronting your parents, you will undoubtedly find the very thought of doing so intimidating. The fears that create this feeling of intimidation are usually the same as, or very similar to, fears that your parents experience! If you can think that you and your parents *share* the same fears, as well as the same conflicts, that will help you to be less critical.

EXERCISE: Deep Down, My Parents Aren't So Different from Me

An empathy-developing exercise you can employ was described by Chade-Meng Tan (2012). He calls it "Just Like Me and Loving Kindness Meditation" (p. 169).

Get into a comfortable position where you will be undisturbed and visualize your parent figures. Then think about each of them as being a person just like you and just like any other person, in that they have at times been sad, disappointed, angry, hurt, or confused. Think that they want to be free of these negative feelings, to be loved, and to have good relationships—again, just like you. As you visualize them as fellow human beings, make a wish for them to be happy. Visualize being kind to them in that way—even when they sometimes misbehave.

Keeping Emotional Distance

One big secret to maintaining an empathic attitude, even when your parents are pushing your buttons, is to learn how to keep a degree of emotional distance while discussing touchy subjects. Learning how to do this will help you to minimize the number of mistakes you make as you struggle to remain in control of shifting the gears while your parents needle you. It will keep you from immediately falling back into old, automatic response patterns.

As you are discussing issues, either while practicing your skills or during actual exchanges with your parents, imagine yourself *watching* the interactions from a distance as if you were watching yourself in a movie. Think about what is happening as if you were watching a chess match rather than participating in a life-or-death struggle. This will help you to act somewhat more dispassionately.

You can think of metacommunicative conversation as a sort of contest in which outwitting your opponents is far more important than expressing your feelings about their mind-set. The big difference between metacommunication and a chess match is that the goal is not for *you* to win, but for *both of you* to win.

Practice Your Tone of Voice

We human beings naturally respond more—and more quickly—to tone of voice and body language than we do to the actual words coming from the mouths of our fellow *Homo sapiens*. The best tone of voice to use during attempts at metacommunication is one that is warm, pleasant, and kind, yet still matter-of-fact. You should also be firm and resolute when it comes to bringing up issues. You want to appear somewhat fearless in this regard. Also helpful is acting somewhat bemused, with an ever-so-slight dose of self-deprecation, while remaining unafraid when it comes to describing your own feelings and reactions.

You do not want to sound like a whiny little child who is not getting his or her way. Also watch out for anything you might say that suggests *sarcasm* or *disdain* and keep it in check. Make certain you are not coming across as a know-it-all who has every right to tell them exactly how they should live their lives. Lecturing them as if they were little children will not get you anywhere. You also do not want to sound remotely like a nag or a scold.

EXERCISE: Landing the Right Tone

Use a camcorder or a smart phone with video capabilities to record yourself while you practice modulating your tone in this manner. Keep practicing until you achieve the desired effect.

Communicate Openness with Body Language

Your body language should be as relaxed as possible. Stand or sit with open and uncrossed arms, and make good eye contact without staring or extensive blinking. Avoid sudden movements or any motions that might be construed as aggressive. Your facial expression should be pleasant yet serious. Lines on your forehead (a "furrowed brow") often indicate annoyance or confusion, so try not to show those except when you are using the strategy of expressing puzzlement, which I'll describe later.

If you're concerned that you'll be focusing on this at the expense of saying what you have to say, listening, and responding, you'll recognize the value of practicing and role-playing in advance so this kind of body ease becomes second nature.

Being Concise Conveys Confidence

When it comes to verbal behavior, metacommunication is generally more effective if you can make your points as concisely as possible, so they don't get lost in a sea of words. This is also important because it helps to avoid overexplaining yourself in ways that might suggest to your parents that you may not feel entirely justified in your opinions or that you are feeling defensive. If they sense this, they can use any extraneous wordage you use as a basis for going off on a tangential discussion of other, only partially related matters. Alternatively, they can feed into any tendencies you may have to feel unsure of yourself. This can also happen if you sound too argumentative, such as by repeating things you have already said. When you start planning your strategy—as will be described in the following chapters—write down your main points ahead of time, phrasing and rephrasing them until they communicate your thoughts and countermoves with simplicity and directness.

Anticipating Parental Defensive Reactions

As you plan how you will make the points you hope to make, ask yourself, *What kind of negative reactions might I get to anything I am considering saying?* and *What have they done or said to me on several occasions in the past that might come into play?*

For every move that you make in the metacommunication process, your parents may have a countermove designed to get you to back off. This is why generic "assertiveness" techniques (Alberti and Emmons 2017) often fail. The key is anticipating and preparing for what might go wrong.

Fallback Strategies When Things Go Wrong

Even after you have devised and practiced the empathic strategies in this chapter, sooner or later during the metacommunication process, you may either hit a wall with your parents or lose your temper and say something decidedly unempathic. If you have already tried unsuccessfully to discuss your parents' problematic behavior, this is bound to happen. It is important to recognize when either of these two eventualities is *starting* to occur so that you can employ a counterstrategy.

You can watch for several early signs indicating that the conversation is headed in the wrong direction. The goal is to prevent the conversation between you and your parents from degenerating even further or scuttling the whole endeavor. Be reassured that, because of the power of the biological forces of attachment between you and your parents, you can go back and correct almost any mistake you make in the metacommunication process.

Here are the three big clues that the process is not going well:

- You have a sense of déjà vu—a feeling that you seem to be repeating a conversation or argument that you all have already had several times in the past.

- You find yourself becoming infuriated, overly anxious or fearful, or completely confused to the point where you feel you are going to lose it and say things that will be quite counterproductive.

- You begin to lose empathy, which can become evident when your parent becomes increasing angry or defensive and starts to intensify her invalidating or hostile behavior.

The last clue is a bit more complicated than the previous two, because as we'll soon discuss, your parent may be feigning these reactions as a *countermove* to something that you had actually done very well. Once you've read chapter 6, you will be able to anticipate your parents' tactics for getting you to be quiet. Then you should be able to figure out whether you are on the right or the wrong track, which will guide your next move.

When these clues begin to emerge, in order to eventually succeed in resolving ongoing issues you will need to *temporarily back off* from the metacommunicative process. For whatever reason, the conversation is becoming unproductive and you need to stop it before it gets even worse. But it is essential to *continue the conversation at a later time.* Giving up is not allowed!

How to Pause the Conversation

Here's a simple strategy for backing off temporarily from a conversation when things start to heat up and you are at risk of not keeping your cool: say "Look, I don't want to fight. Let me think about this some more and *get back to you about it later.*" This response does not reward the parental behavior that led you to call a time-out. By "reward," I mean increasing the likelihood your parent will repeat that behavior to get you to be quiet. That's why it's absolutely essential to add that "get back to you about it later"; if you don't, you may trigger a process called an "intermittent reinforcement schedule." Your parents may think to themselves (although not necessarily in these words), *Aha! I now know exactly what to do to get the kid to shut up. If she starts up again, I'll just do that again!*

If your parent still insists on continuing the conversation, or escalates even further after you have called for a time-out, I suggest adding, "Look, I am not going to talk to you about this until I have a chance to think about it." A kind but very firm tone is again vitally important. If your parent keeps going on and on, leave the room. If you are on the phone, say that you are going to hang up, and then do it.

Following this advice can be infinitely more difficult for you if you happen to live with your parents. They can then follow you into another room and keep berating you. In response, you might have to leave the house and take a walk. If they resume the minute you get back home, turn around and go take another walk. Eventually they will get the message that you mean business. Alternatively, you can metaphorically turn to stone by refusing to reply to them no matter what they say, and just staring at them intently.

Think Through the Conversation

After backing off, as soon as possible, find some place you can be alone, then write down the entire conversation as best as you can remember it. Examine the conversation in detail and in chronological order to best figure out what went wrong and what you could do differently the next time. Your recounting should include, if at all possible, descriptions of how the conversation got started and exactly how it started to head south.

Study what you have written and try to figure out what you or your parents may have been reacting to that might have either led you to start losing empathy or led them to become increasingly defensive, or both. Then look through this book for a different strategy that might get you back on track. Once again, think about any past parental behavior that might help you anticipate how they might react negatively to your next idea, and prepare yourself for it by practicing the appropriate countermoves offered in the next two chapters.

For now, let us turn to the question of what you should do if you do lose control of yourself and say something negative, hostile, demeaning, insulting, or sarcastic. What then?

The Fine Art of Apology

As soon as you realize that you have lost empathy and gone on the attack, quickly end the conversation with, "Look, this isn't going the way I hoped. Let me think about this and get back to you later." Then find a way to be alone, calm down, and think things through. *After* both you and your parent have calmed down, go back, own up to your mistake, and apologize for it! Be a person of integrity. Be someone who is responsible, has a sense of right and wrong, and is the sort of person others can look up to.

It's essential that you apologize *only for what you actually said or did*, but *not* for the feelings that led to it. Your feelings were perfectly valid, and saying they were not would be invalidating yourself. Furthermore, apologizing for your feelings rather than for your behavior would give your parents the message that you think their unreasonable behavior was not all that problematic, and that no one but you was out of line.

In this situation, your apology should not have *the slightest hint of self-denigration* attached to it. If you put yourself down in some way, your parents may then go for the jugular. Be good-natured about your error. After all, you are only human. Be able to laugh at yourself, as in "Gee, I sure did get frustrated with you that time." Here are some examples.

- "I am sorry I snapped at you—I know it wasn't the first time—but I just had the feeling that you were dismissing everything I said out of hand."

- "I'm sorry I called you a bitch. That was really out of line— but man, you sure were pissing me off."

- "I apologize, Dad. I took some time to think about what you were really saying, and while how you said it hurt, I get the underlying message now."

These apologies have the positive effect of framing the explosive interchange as a *mutual* problem that the two of you need to work to solve in a constructive manner. And, after all, solving interpersonal problems is what effective metacommunication is all about. When it comes to metacommunication, no mistake you make need be fatal, because you always have the balm of apology at your disposal.

Getting everyone in the family to open up about conflictual issues and to explore alternative ways of dealing with them is not easy. If it were, there would be no need for a book like this. You need to keep at it. Additionally, if a strategy you have chosen is not working, do not become a model for Einstein's definition of insanity by repeating it over and over again with the same bad result; instead, try to figure out why the strategy is not working, then try a different one. Your parents' multiple resistances to your efforts represent multiple problems to be solved, not multiple reasons for giving up!

As I discuss problematic parental responses and effective countermoves in the following chapters, think about whether or not your parents have used them on you. At the end of chapter 6, you will do an exercise to further develop your ability to anticipate your parents' typical moves.

CHAPTER 5

Keep the Logic Straight

Your problematic parent may tend to use irrational arguments and logical fallacies to throw you off track when you attempt to constructively discuss her behavior. Playing with logic is used as a defensive tactic designed to frighten, mislead, or anger you. It can create confusion so that you do not know how to respond, and so that you will discontinue your attempt at metacommunication. It is an invalidating move, because people who use it seem to be saying that you are the one being illogical or ridiculous, not them. Sometimes the lack of reasonableness is so convoluted that I refer to it as "mental gymnastics."

Mental gymnastics are also used to maintain some fiction that justifies counterproductive family rules and behavior patterns. In maintaining family rules, it is amazing how people cling to ideas and propositions they absolutely must know make no sense. We all do this automatically to some degree. But they can be successfully challenged.

By prepping yourself to be able to identify logical tricks and keeping ways to counter them at the ready, you can approach your metacommunication with confidence and clarity. Do not—I repeat, do not—allow yourself to be drawn into an extended argument. If you do, your parent will almost invariably double down on his own illogical position with a version of the old saw, "My mind is made up; don't confuse me with the facts."

Assume Your Parents Are Capable of Reason

Shortly, I will give case examples involving some of the most commonly used logical fallacies and strategies for countering them. To successfully employ the countermoves, your best weapon is your own attitude. You need to *assume* that everybody is capable of logical thought, and that your parents can be induced to discuss a situation in a rational manner. This applies no matter how unreasonable they appear to be at the outset, and despite your having been exposed to a long history of evidence to the contrary.

Because of your long and ongoing interactions with your parents, believing they are capable of more logical thinking may seem like a stretch. Recall, however, what good actors they have to be in order to maintain family rules that run counter to their own interests, and to convince not only themselves but everyone else that they really do believe all the nonsense they sometimes spout. If you can assume in an empathic way that they simply *must* know better underneath, often this will induce them to stop and think more objectively about what they are saying, as well as to start considering their real feelings about any rules that you are calling into question.

Ways Your Parents Might Play with Logic

To help you spot illogical statements when you hear them, as well as to provide you with additional countermoves, I will now briefly review some of the best-known and most frequently used logical fallacies, and the family issues they are most frequently used to obfuscate.

Non Sequiturs

"*I read that your generation feels entitled. You kids just don't appreciate everything I do for you!*"

A non sequitur is a conclusion or statement that does not logically follow from the previous argument or statement. In this example, it does not follow that just because you are part of a certain generation you absolutely must share some characteristic that is frequently seen in that group (this is also called the "ecological fallacy"). Within any classification of people there will always be many individuals who do not share a prevalent characteristic. Parents might use this fallacy to change the subject from the complaint you are making about their behavior to whether your complaint is invalid because it is really just some manifestation of a quirk in your personality. If you allow them to get away with this, the opportunity to question the real reasons for their behavior—so you can discuss the ambivalence about family rules that leads to it—is completely lost.

Misty's Story: Being Oversensitive, Rather Than Wronged

Misty's mother, Marcella, was very critical whenever Misty complained about anything, teasing her about it or calling her "oversensitive." Marcella did hold herself to the same standard: she could be very self-denigrating. In a seemingly unrelated discussion, the mother had complained about how she herself was frequently being subjected to sexually harassing comments by her boss. This had been going on almost every day for a year, despite the fact that Marcella had apparently done nothing to indicate that she had any romantic interest in him at all. She opined that she should be able to blow off his behavior like water off a duck's back since he never threatened her job if she did not submit to his advances. She seemed highly upset with herself for being upset by his behavior.

Then came the non sequitur: Marcella said that the fact that boss could upset her "so easily" meant that she was a weak, inadequate snowflake, and she needed to work on becoming more resilient. Misty thought that did not make sense; from her standpoint, anyone would be upset after being harassed in the manner that Marcella was being subjected to and, if her circumstances allowed her to consider leaving, would probably be actively looking for another job. She herself would have been even more upset than her mother was in that situation, and for her to just laugh it off it would require almost superhuman strength. She was reasonably certain that it was illogical to label being bothered by sexual harassment as some sort of personality flaw.

Misty's Countermove

As a countermove, Misty simply disagreed that Marcella's being upset about her torment meant she was weak, and she expressed puzzlement that her mom was being so hard on herself. Out of nowhere, Marcella mentioned in passing a clue to what was really going on with her. Without any prompting, she began to reminisce. She had long been puzzled why everyone seemed to think that her own parents' divorce had traumatized her. She added that she had been able to easily take the divorce in stride. It was done, and therefore there was no reason to get upset about it. Misty thought to herself, Yeah, right. She knew better.

Wisely keeping with the overall recommended strategies, Misty temporarily dropped the discussion of her mother's logic and went along with the sudden revelation: "Really? Tell me more about that." Marcella then revealed that her mother (Misty's grandmother) had subjected her to frequent guilt-ridden harangues about how bad she felt about the divorce. Grandma would badger Marcella with questions about whether she, as their daughter, had been upset and traumatized by it. No wonder Marcella tried to force herself to project an image of not being bothered by things! If she had admitted to being the least bit upset, her mother would have felt even guiltier. Her mother was already somewhat self-destructive; when she was disturbed, she sometimes threatened suicide.

On further questioning, Misty learned that her grandmother had been disowned by her own parents after her divorce. The family was strongly against divorce in any context, despite the fact that the grandfather was a philandering alcoholic. Obtaining this genogram information—which came out unexpectedly, and about which Marcella had previously said nothing—allowed Misty to understand why her mother felt so threatened by the sensitivity she saw in both Misty and herself. Misty thought it likely that her grandmother felt quite guilty about upsetting her own parents with her divorce, so she may have projected that guilt onto Marcella, whom she was afraid she had harmed as well. Marcella was following a seeming mandate from her mother to appear to be unbothered by anything. An empathic discussion between Misty and Marcella followed, in which Misty empathized with why her mother was beating herself up. This allowed a frank discussion about the effects that her mother's frequent criticisms had on Misty—and the frequency of such criticisms soon decreased dramatically.

Post Hoc Fallacy

"So you dislike your new job even more than the perfectly good one you quit. You thought you could do better? That's what you get for chasing rainbows."

The complete Latin logical fallacy is *Post hoc ergo propter hoc*; literally translated, it means "afterward this, therefore because of this." According to this fallacy, two events that occur in sequence are assumed to be causally related. That is, if event B follows event A, then it's assumed that A caused B. That is itself a non sequitur. It is akin to saying that, for example, since penicillin can cure infections, then people must get infections in the first place because their bodies do not produce enough penicillin.

When spotted in metacommunicative discussions, the use of this fallacy may reveal the presence of a family myth or an individual defense mechanism. Your parents use it to suppress their unacceptable thoughts, feelings, preferences, or behavior that get in the way of continuing to fulfill a specific family function, as described in chapter 1. Post hoc statements can also be used to avoid facing a conflict by providing a causal explanation for a family member's problematic behavior that is not the *true* explanation.

Jake's Story: Suddenly Too Busy

Jake had moved out of the family home, and his workaholic father, Kevin, was withdrawing from him and losing interest in Jake's activities—particularly in his career. His father had seemed to go from one extreme to the other—from micromanaging Jake's day while he was in high school to now seeming totally uninterested.

When Jake was in high school, his mother had deserted the family. Kevin tried to be both mother and father to his two sons while working long hours. Kevin worked for a firm that continually demanded more and more overtime, but Kevin never complained. He did his best to almost try to be in two places at once. He looked overburdened and exhausted, but he always took care of everything and everybody without complaint. In fact, he tried to supervise his two sons' every move.

Jake had moved out as soon as he could; he was tired of Kevin's trying to run his life while at the same time seeming overburdened and somewhat depressed about it. When he first moved out, whenever he called to talk to his father, Kevin was brusque, got off the phone quickly, and seemed irritated whenever Jake talked about his new job. Kevin would say he had things he needed to do for Jake's brother. Jake initially reacted to this by calling less frequently.

Eventually, Jake asked Kevin why he seemed to be ignoring him. Kevin acted surprised. He stammered and seemed to reach for excuses. Finally, he said, "I've been extra busy working overtime, and I figured you're busy with the new job and want to be left alone." While this seemed reasonable on the surface and certainly was factually correct, it was not the real explanation. Kevin had worked a lot of overtime many times over the course of Jake's upbringing, and that had never stopped him from being involved with Jake at any of those other times. To Jake, the logic just didn't match Kevin's actions.

Jake's Countermove

The family myth that Kevin was operating under, and about which he was highly ambivalent, was that taking care of young children should take precedence over anything else in life that a father might want to do. He believed he had to make as much money as possible to support them in style, as well as make guiding their lives an all-encompassing priority to the exclusion of most everything else. Since this involved sacrificing his other interests and desires, he covertly resented having to do that. However, that resentment made him feel guilty. In reality, he felt bad about the fact that he was now neglecting Jake as well as guilty about the resentment he felt toward his burdens. Additionally, he was completely exhausted from his years as a single father. In response, now that Jake was out on his own, Kevin was subconsciously avoiding him.

Jake also noticed that when Kevin said he had been working a lot of overtime, it sounded as if Kevin was complaining about it. Jake, trying to switch the focus of the conversation to what he suspected was the real issue, first tried being empathic with his dad's exhaustion. "Well, you certainly have worked a lot of overtime over the years to make sure we had everything we needed; I really appreciate that. You must be really wiped out, though."

Kevin did not react well to this. He suddenly changed the subject, firing back, "Well, you haven't exactly been chomping at the bit to spend time with us since you moved out!"

Knowing his father's past pattern of responding, Jake had anticipated that his dad might have a negative reaction to a mention of his being exhausted all the time. Again, part of the *role he played was to never complain about that. And Jake actually had been avoiding Kevin. But the problem would hang over their relationship like a sword if it was not worked through, so Jake persisted with his strategy.*

"Yeah, Dad, I have. And that was because you always seemed tired and irritable whenever I called."

"Well, there is a lot on my plate, but that's what fathers are for. I'm fine; I'm doing what I want to do. You don't have to worry about me!"

Jake then brought up something he knew about his dad's past that seemed to possibly suggest that Kevin was not as happy in his role as he seemed to be indicating, without stating what his observation might mean regarding how his father really felt. "Didn't you once tell me that you were in a band before you got married? Don't you ever miss having time for stuff like that?"

His dad was silent for a while, but the issue that was creating tension between father and son had now been successfully broached. Awareness of the issue made the search for alternatives to their situation possible.

Begging the Question

"Doing that is wrong because that's what our minister told me!"

A person begging the question is insisting that an assertion is proved without offering any proof at all. If someone offers some evidence that the assertion is false, the "beggar" states that the evidence must be incorrect. After all, since the assertion is true, any evidence to the contrary must be faulty. It might seem that the absurdity of this kind of reasoning should be obvious when it occurs, but it can be quite subtle. Often an intervening argument for the questionable assertion is made by the beggar, which is then refuted. The beggar then offers yet another argument, which in turn is refuted. This process continues until the beggar suddenly announces that she has won the case by restating the initial unproved assertion.

Begging the question in metacommunication is seen most often when parents are being questioned about their motivation for some act or acts and do not wish to reveal their true reasons, perhaps even to themselves, because of a dysfunctional role that they are playing. They may assert that they behave in the way they do because that is how they truly wish to behave or because they have no other options. If you present evidence that the behavior seems to be bringing them a great deal of grief or offer them other options, they will either just ignore what you said, invalidate it by making a snide comment, engage in a game of "Why don't you? Yes, but" (getting you to offer suggestions for solving problems they complain about, but then finding something wrong with each and every suggestion), or begin the process of making further refutable arguments and then returning to the initial assertion as if it had been justified.

Brianna's Story: Facing Depression-Era Standards

Brianna and her father, Tyler, were often at odds about Brianna's frequent decisions to change jobs, for reasons that were never clear. Brianna would routinely look for higher-paying or more prestigious jobs and interview with other firms while employed, and when a better opportunity arose, quickly give notice at her current job. She was actually quite successful at improving her income and prospects for advancement with this behavior. She purposely did not change jobs more than once every two years to avoid appearing unreliable. Tyler nonetheless repeatedly criticized her for doing this. Strangely, however, Tyler appeared to be proud of his daughter's ability to navigate her career when he bragged about her to friends.

Tyler, a poorly educated man, worked for a large manufacturing concern. Despite his lack of schooling, he had managed to rise to a fairly responsible position. He then had been assigned to a new supervisor who felt that Tyler really did not have the education required by the job and did not deserve his salary. The supervisor demoted him and made his work life miserable.

Because of her pent-up annoyance at her father's criticisms about her changing jobs, Brianna started questioning him in a somewhat nonempathic manner about why Tyler was so wedded to his current job when he was so miserable. Tyler would not so much as even look for other career opportunities, and Brianna pressed him for a reason for his inactivity. Tyler replied, "Because I love working for this firm." He said he loved it because of the way they used to treat him. Brianna pointed out that this was no longer the case. Tyler then offered a backup explanation: "I want to get in twenty-five years with the firm." He admitted, however, that even then he would probably stay where he was.

Brianna became more frustrated with these illogical responses, so Tyler came up with another backup explanation: "I don't want to give my supervisors the satisfaction of driving me out." This assertion did not make any more sense than the first. Why would avoiding making them smug be worth daily torture at their hands? Not only that, but Tyler admitted that they wouldn't really care all that much if he did leave.

"So why stay?" Brianna asked.

"I've told you. The firm is very important to me. I love working for the firm."

The last statement was, of course, merely a return to Tyler's initial position that did nothing whatever to shed light on why the firm was so important to him. This is exactly what is meant by begging the question.

COUNTERMOVES FOR BEGGING THE QUESTION: ADDITIONAL CONSIDERATIONS

When questions are being begged or leading to "Yes, but" responses, the strategy of offering a hypothesis based on what you have learned from the genogram is often far more effective than continuing to merely ask questions. This is true because, in human interactions, certain types of statements and questions seem to require certain responses. The other person feels obligated to follow the rules of social etiquette and respond in ways that are more enlightening or clear. When presented with a hypothesis, people often feel it's necessary to explain *what is wrong or right* with the hypothesis, rather than just responding yes, no, or I don't know.

You can also increase the odds for this by overtly labeling the hypothesis as a *guess*, thereby giving your parents an out. They can just reject the guess if they are feeling too threatened to respond with more information or if it is just plain wrong. It's essential to avoid any semblance of a power struggle between you and your parent over the accuracy of the hypothesis.

Another countermove to a "Yes, but" is to not offer any more suggestions. If your parent is continually complaining about his situation but finding something wrong with any and every solution anyone suggests for getting out of it, consider that if you have quickly thought of a potential solution, it is probably something pretty obvious. Therefore, your parent has doubtless already thought of it. Instead of trying to solve the problem, you might instead say something like, "It sounds like a tough situation, but you're pretty resourceful. I'm sure you could come up with a way out if you put your mind to it." Most parents will be loath to argue that they are really too impaired to do that. But if they do, refuse to argue the point, and perhaps give them a puzzled look.

Brianna's Countermove

In thinking about a countermove, Brianna drew from what she had learned through researching the family history. Her father had come of age near the end of the Great Depression, when jobs were scarce and at a premium. He had often been unemployed, and poverty was an ever-present concern. In fact, the reason for Tyler's lack of schooling was that he had to drop out to help support the family, and the firm he now worked for had been his only option. His own father had lectured him repeatedly about doing whatever he had to do to keep any job, because there might not be another available and the family could starve.

Brianna went back to her father and said, "I don't know if this applies to you or not, but in other families from the Depression era, jobs were scarce and people had to do whatever they could to keep them. They could not afford to quit one even if they hated it. Of course, the economy is much better now, but I wonder if you still react as if the old rules you had to live by still apply?"

Tyler looked somewhat surprised. After thinking about what she'd said, he replied, "I guess I never thought about it that way."

The Worst-Case Argument

"I have to check up on you every day; what if something happened and you weren't able to get to a phone?"

A parent arguing that a particular course of action that you want to take (or she wants to take) is ill-advised may point out difficulties that might arise in a worst-case scenario. She asks, "If you did so and so, what would be the consequences if everything that could possibly go wrong did go wrong?" Posing a worst-case scenario does not always mean that the poser is engaged in an illogical maneuver. Indeed, for certain actions that may have life-or-death consequences, anticipating worst-case scenarios may be crucial.

The worst-case argument becomes logically suspect *if* it is being used as an excuse to avoid some action when either of two conditions is present: the worst case is so unlikely to occur as to be almost meaningless, or the worst case is easily preventable.

The example in the heading—what might happen if you can't get to a phone?—has clearly become absurd in the age of cell phones, but even if you did not have one, it still does not make sense. If something happened to you, what are the odds that your parent would happen to reach you in time to help you? And if you were not close by, how could they come to your assistance quickly enough? Also, the statement is insulting. Why does your mom think that you cannot take care of yourself?

This parental maneuver most commonly involves their suppression of unacceptable feelings—again, either yours, the parent's own, or both. Your parent attempts to suppress some tempting desires by frightening himself with the thought of dreadful consequences should he ever act on those desires. If he is projecting his conflict onto you, he will attempt to scare you out of breaking the family rule about self-expression by predicting a horrible aftermath if you do so. His constant warnings may then feed into your own unrealistic anxieties.

Wyatt's Story: Fearing Endless Wrath

Wyatt's parents employed a family myth that is one of the most common examples of the use of this fallacy. No members were allowed to stand up for themselves when they were being taken advantage of, and anger over being mistreated thusly was suppressed, using this fallacy as justification. In fact, any expression of anger by anyone in his family was immediately met with relentless criticism from everyone else. Family members would often scare themselves into passivity by warning one another of the most shocking and dire results that might ensue if their anger was ever unleashed. They might murder loved ones or become a terrorist, and they'd end up spending the rest of their lives in prison. If dire warnings like that do not scare someone into keeping anger in check, nothing will.

This worst-case scenario is illogical for two main reasons. First, it posits a highly unlikely conclusion "If I let out some of my anger, I'll completely lose control and become a raving maniac." People can almost always rein themselves in. In fact, people who suppress their anger are often masters at doing just that, despite the fact that stuffing your anger is more likely to finally lead to a violent explosion than letting it out a little at a time. Furthermore, this worse case is preventable. Acting it out is hardly the only way to express one's anger.

Wyatt's Countermove

In Wyatt's case, he was able to directly challenge the family's justification for the family myth. The fact that they were all highly capable of self-restraint was just too obvious to argue with. The next time the issue was raised, Wyatt smiled and warmly replied, "I am pretty sure you don't have to worry about that. I am actually more concerned that we all don't get angry enough when we should—that instead we just sit there, not speaking up, and let things eat away at us. That can't be good."

When he said this, his parents had no answer, and fell silent. He was then able to go on and bring up a hypothesis about why the family was so freaked out about standing up for themselves.

Going Beyond the False Logic: Overarching Strategies

Now that you know about the specific logical fallacies, and you have considered the stories that illustrate how the strategies might unfold, let's look at more general strategies for countering them.

Upon being confronted with an illogical explanation for a problem or for the motivation of a family member, the initial countermove is to point out a seeming error in the parent's reasoning in a reassuring, nonjudgmental way. You might, for example, bring up facts or observations that seemingly contradict your parent's assertion. To avoid sounding too argumentative, you should do this without directly saying very much about what your observations might mean.

Another option is to suggest an alternative explanation for your parents' consideration. This might include references to historical problems for the family that you discovered while doing your genogram. In fact, bringing up your own, alternative hypothesis about the reasons for your parents' behavior instead of directly challenging their explanation can serve as a launching point for a far more extensive discussion about what you think might be the covert, underlying issue.

When countering an illogical statement in this manner, again, it is essential to use a calm, matter-of-fact tone of voice. You should act as if you are assuming that your parent had made the illogical statement innocently—that she was just not thinking clearly at that point or perhaps had merely neglected to think about the evidence that contradicts the idea, despite how obvious it was. Had your parent thought about it, she would have taken it into account and would never have made the illogical statement. Again, do not be argumentative with her.

If you approach this as recommended here, parents will generally respond in one of four possible ways:

Agreeing with You

They might respond in a positive way. If they agree that their explanation does not hold up, invite them to join in a search for a better one.

Suddenly Switching to the Underlying Issue

They might surprise you by suddenly dropping the entire subject of the reasonableness of the argument in question and launching into a discussion of what you really wanted to discuss in the first place—the real, underlying reasons for their behavior or the family history behind it. (This will be illustrated shortly with Misty's story.)

If this happens, rather than resuming your focus on the illogical reasoning, go ahead and let it drop. However, the argument you had been having about the fallacy will feel unfinished, so you might be strongly tempted to return to it. Resist that temptation by reminding yourself that the underlying issue is exactly what you wanted to get to all along!

Insisting You're Wrong (So You'll Need to Learn More)

They might react by pointing out the error in *your* reasoning. Perhaps you were the one who was not thinking straight, or perhaps you were not aware of a relevant fact that would have altered your ideas about the matter being discussed. In fact, in this situation, your countermove may lead you to discover something new and important about your family that puts your problem with your parent in a whole different light. In keeping with previous recommendations, if and when that happens, *admit your error* in a nondefensive tone of voice, then try to find out more about these new discoveries.

Building Fallacy upon Fallacy

Despite your nonargumentative approach, parents may dig in their heels even further in their role of "illogical person." They might augment an explanation with an even more farfetched argument than the one they had already given, or they may just pout and insist they are right. This sort of behavior does not prove that they are fundamentally irrational. I cannot emphasize too strongly that you must convey the attitude that you *know* they can do better.

In this situation I advise responding by *expressing puzzlement*. You might say, "I don't understand why you are saying this when I know you understand what is wrong with it" or "I'm confused by your reaction. I know you understand what I just said, but you seem to be ignoring it."

Family members use logical fallacies so they can maintain ambivalently held group norms and follow problematic family rules. These are also defensive maneuvers designed to prevent you from challenging them. In the next chapter, we will look at a wide variety of other strategies that your parents may employ against you to stop you when you attempt to challenge the problematic rules, as well as effective counterstrategies you can apply to keep problem-solving discussions of family dynamics on track.

CHAPTER 6

Anticipate the Seventeen Moves They May Make and Plan Your Countermoves

Your parents likely employ a variety of strategies to get you to stop talking about difficult subjects. In metacommunication, people often use ambiguous and invalidating language when talking about conflictual feelings, beliefs, and motives. They do not want you to know how they really feel or think, and they may also be deathly afraid of admitting how they feel, even to themselves. Ambiguous responses *seem* to address the matter at hand but really do not address it much at all. They may also be so confusing to you that you cannot figure out where to go next. Invalidating responses disparage your feelings and ideas as foolish or crazy.

In this chapter, we will discuss seventeen strategies your parents may use to undermine or derail your efforts to clarify issues to be able to resolve them or at least explore new ways of relating. Read through all of these, recalling previous interactions while beginning to look for those that continue to take place in the present. At the end of the chapter, you can prepare your countermoves—but again, don't apply them until you are familiar with all of the metacommunication skills offered here and in the rest of this book.

1. Misleading Judgments

If your parents are constantly critical of a particular thing that you do, or a trait that you have, they may be characterizing your behavior using adjectives with negative connotations. A connotation is the feeling that a word evokes in you on top of its literal or primary meaning. For every quality we can ascribe to people, there is an applicable adjective with a negative value connotation and another applicable adjective with a positive connotation. Someone can be stubborn or determined, loyal or a sycophant, self-confident or arrogant, and so forth.

When parents use one of these adjectives, they may choose one with a particular connotation to mask either their distaste for *or* their admiration for the quality in question. But which one? They may want that connotation of the word they chose to apply to you to conceal their true opinions about the matter at hand. For instance, Janis's mother criticized her for vocalizing her need for things to change with coworkers. When Janis asked why that bothered her so much, her mother responded with, "You're so controlling!" This implies that Janis has been doing something bad, because the adjective "controlling" is usually applied to someone who is unreasonable or doing something undesirable.

Countermove: *Follow-Up Questions*

Follow-up questions are useful here; you can also use them at any point in metacommunication to force someone to be clearer about what precisely they are saying. In a polite and pleasant tone of voice, you can ask your parent to be *more specific* about *exactly* what they mean when they say something that could be interpreted in many different ways. Follow-up questions Janis might ask include:

- "Why is it a bad thing to speak up, when our business may be harmed if I don't?"

- "What are you mostly concerned about?"

- "Did you ever find yourself in a real pickle because *you* spoke up about something?"

- "Did Grandpa preach that women should always be subservient?"

These types of questions raise the possibility that you and your parents might behave in ways that run counter to family rules—and that is precisely what you want to discuss. It can lead to a discussion of the consequences they are so afraid of. What might Janis's mother be afraid of happening if she were to speak out? Is there a family rule that "rocking the boat means everyone will fall overboard," originating at a time when the family had to flee Europe due to their great-grandfather's outspokenness? Is she scaring herself with illogical thoughts that Janis is bound to lose her job no matter how she phrases her concerns there?

Another concern here—and keeping this in mind can help you to remain empathic—is that parents often use misleading judgments and other strategies out of shame and embarrassment over their own thoughts and feelings. Janis's mother may be worried, for example, that Janis will think less of her if she admits to feeling bad over her lack of assertiveness, as well as the fact that she was a coward when it came to breaking the family rule.

2. Describing Instead of Explaining

This phenomenon often comes into play when you are attempting to obtain an undistorted or honest explanation of a parent's conscious motives for engaging in a particular course of action. Instead of communicating the actual reasoning behind his choice, he may instead merely describe his state of mind at the time of the action. This response *sounds* like an explanation for his motives or fears but in fact explains absolutely nothing.

This type of statement can be a dodge to avoid admitting something. Ten-year-old Mike's father offered an illustrative example of this with his statement: "I won't go gawk at holiday lights, because I just don't like them." There are always two types of reasons why someone does or does not "want" or "like" to do something, and in these cases the person is not indicating exactly which of the two is in play.

The first type of reason is based on idiosyncratic taste. There is no accounting for it; just as some people prefer blue suits to black suits, your father thinks holiday lights are ugly. However, when a family member claims to base his decision to choose or avoid a course of action on a mere personal idiosyncrasy, he may be avoiding the real reason.

The second type is a preference based on feared consequences. For example, Mike's father, Doug, may say that he hates holiday lights and does not even like to go look at them because if he doesn't say so, Mike will continue to push him to put some up on their two-story house; Mike does not know his father is afraid of heights, and his father is ashamed to admit to this. This shame developed because his own father, Mike's grandfather, used to tease Doug relentlessly about his phobia.

When someone is ambivalent about family rules, she may use this type of misleading explanation to explain away problematic acts such as frequently and compulsively teasing you or doing things to avoid intimacy. In almost all cases of complex behavior, a decision like that is far more likely to be motivated by the second type of reason—feared consequences—than by the first. It is based on past negative or frightening experiences with that course of action, whether created by their family or by the outside world through which they have navigated.

Countermove: *Follow-Up Questions*

When you hear your parents say that their motives for complex, repetitive behavior are based on simple likes or dislikes, you can safely assume that they have experienced unintended adverse consequences whenever they made the seemingly "healthier" choice. For example, Nora's mother refuses to go to school to get retrained in a new occupation after an on-the-job injury halted her previous career. She explains her decision by saying, "I just don't like school." Nora can counter by asking her specifically what she thinks might happen if she were to go back to school. Such questions include:

- What are the pluses and minuses about school that make you feel the way you do?

- What makes you give a lot of weight to some of them and little weight to others?

- Are any feared consequences of going to school sufficiently onerous to account for your dislike?

- How likely are they to actually occur in the present?

- If something could be done about the consequences, would you want to make a different choice? And if so, why have you avoided remedying the situation?

Parents may have a backup explanation that is also a dodge because the feared consequence of certain actions that they give is just not significant or powerful enough to really explain their apparently self-defeating behavior. A common one is the "single traumatic event hypothesis"—when a past traumatic experience that seems almost comically trivial or commonplace is described as the sole reason for avoiding a course of action. Nora's mother said she was just "uncomfortable in classrooms"—all because of an incident in which her seventh-grade English teacher embarrassed her in front of the class. The problem with this "explanation" is that just about everyone was embarrassed by his or her seventh-grade English teacher at one time or another. While the event probably had something to do with her apparent aversion to school, there just had to be something more than that to cause what appeared to be a full-blown school phobia. The extent of her "trauma" was in no way commensurate with a fear so all-encompassing that she seemed to be prepared to live a life of poverty rather than get retrained. Follow-up questions here might include:

- Did something else happen after he embarrassed you?

- How did your parents react to what your teacher did?

- What seems to make you focus only on this event?

- Why do you think you have been unable to recover from it?

- What have you done to try to overcome the problem, and if nothing, why?

If your parent replies to the final question with "I just didn't think there was anything I could do about it," ask if your parent has even looked into possible solutions, and if not, why not.

3. Flat-Out Contradictions

As a conversation progresses, a parent may communicate two contradictory ideas, while ignoring their possible inconsistency (Allen 1991). It will appear that he either has not thought about the two ideas at the same time or has avoided putting one right next to the other so that the obvious contradiction might arise for questioning and clarification.

Lisa's father compulsively expresses the idea that the biggest satisfaction in his entire life has been his current job with the only company he has ever worked for, but he also frequently complains about how he has hated his boss and coworkers ever since he started working there. He may make such contradictory statements days or even weeks apart. You may have to think long and hard about prior conversations to recall these inconsistent claims.

In the same vein, your parent may say something in a way that seems to imply that you perhaps should have some doubt as to exactly what she meant. She just does not seem completely committed to an idea or she seems to be avoiding her true opinions. This maneuver prevents other people from holding the speaker accountable for any particular sentiment. This can be done in any of three ways:

- Damning with faint praise. Your mother might say, "You're so economical," after opening a handmade gift.

- Using qualifiers like "strictly" or "completely." Your father might say, "The aunt who raised me was not, strictly speaking, very friendly."

- Negating with nonverbal communication. As your uncle says, "My sister was always an angel, a model of morality," he rolls his eyes slightly, inviting you to question the apparent truthfulness or the tenor of what he said.

In all of these cases, the listener is forced to guess what the speaker really means.

Your parents could also be obviously seeking to have it both ways. They may unceasingly describe the pros and cons of a particular viewpoint or course of action without ever saying what they really believe or making a decision about what to do. They may continuously vacillate in their opinion about an issue.

Your parents' moods may be similarly changeable. They may quickly plunge from the heights of ecstasy to the depths of despair about the same issue, which leaves you uncertain about how they actually feel. Or you can never pin down their take on someone, as they shift from idealization to denigration.

With all of these behaviors, your parents avoid clearly stating their true beliefs and opinions—most likely in order to avoid confronting any secret desire to break or alter a family role that has been assigned to them.

Countermove: *Express Puzzlement*

Instead of getting angry about the contradictions, or accusing your parents of having ulterior motives or trying to confuse you, a powerful tactic is to ask your parents for their *help* so you can better understand them. In doing so, assign any confusion to yourself rather than to them: it's not that *they* are unclear; it's *you* who just cannot quite get it. This maneuver has been deemed the "*Columbo* style of questioning," named after the fictional TV detective who would often elicit a confession from a suspect by acting stupid and asking the suspect to "help him understand" something by clarifying an inconsistency or a contradiction.

Lisa might say, "I know that you say your job is the best thing in your life, and then later you said your bosses have always been whining incompetents. I seem to be missing something. Did I hear you right?" When her father responds with a proverb—"Well, the devil you know is always better than the devil you don't"—Lisa is clued in that a possible family myth that she does not know about might be governing her father's choices. Now she can begin to understand why her father has always been so critical of her whenever she wanted to do something new.

When using this strategy, I cannot overemphasize the importance of tone of voice and phrasing. Saying something like, "Why can't you make up your damned mind?" or "Stop trying to confuse me!" is not going to elicit the desired information. You should instead use a sort of bemused tone of voice and self-deprecating style. Even if the parent responds with, "What are you, stupid?" you can reply almost sheepishly, "Could be, but I just don't get it."

4. Becoming Defensive or Hostile for No Apparent Reason

When you are trying to get parents to open up about why they persist with difficult behaviors with you, despite your frequent objections, they may suddenly become defensive or hostile. They may seem to be trying to infuriate you, and you won't be able to figure out exactly why. They might start accusing you of being insensitive, paranoid, stupid, or unappreciative of their efforts to help you run your life. They might even say you are making up things that you can use against them because you are some sort of bad seed. They can become offended that you would dare talk to them in the way you are talking, despite your attempts to be both empathic and conciliatory.

Countermove: *Verbalize Rather Than Act Out*

A major principle of metacommunication is that calmly *verbalizing your feelings* is far better than *acting them out*. If parents say something that makes you furious, yelling and swearing at them in response will of course be counterproductive. Instead, you can tell them as nicely and quietly as possible that you felt angry when they said it. Therapists who teach assertiveness techniques (Alberti and Emmons 2017) recommend the use of so-called *I-messages*. People are advised to say "I respond with X when you do Y" rather than saying "You *make me* feel such-and-such a way." Note that "When you do that, I think you're a jerk" is not this type of I-message.

To verbalize feelings and express puzzlement, use the following basic structure: "You know, when you react [in the way that you are now reacting], I feel [angry, annoyed, helpless, like dropping this whole conversation]. This subject is very important to me, and I think it is important in our relationship. I know you care about me, so *I don't understand why* you are reacting so [negatively, angrily]. What is it about what I am saying that's so [irritating, troublesome]?"

If your parent then continues to lash out at you by dismissing your observations out of hand without refuting them, or continues to behave in the same unpleasant way, you can counter by placing that new response into *the same category as the parent's initial response*. You might say, "When you ignore the point I am trying to make and continue on as if I had said nothing, I find it extremely annoying. I still do not understand why you keep doing that."

Countermove: *Express Puzzlement*

You can also use the *Columbo* line of questioning here. Calmly describe your emotional reactions, and then go on to express—from the "one down" position of just not being smart enough to figure it out—your confusion about why your parent is being so hostile. As in the case of Lisa, or of Misty and Marcella in chapter 5, your parent may blurt out something you hadn't considered before that gets closer to the heart of the matter.

Countermove: *Disclaimers*

Disclaimers are introductory statements that acknowledge the potentially unpleasant nature of the issue at hand, which nonetheless needs to be discussed further, while proclaiming the lack of any ill intent on your part (Allen 2003). Using disclaimers decreases the likelihood that your parents will continue to be defensive—or even get defensive in the first place—while increasing the likelihood that they will consider the merits of any ideas you suggest. Here are some examples.

BENEFIT OF THE DOUBT

You want to bring up your parents' irritating behavior, and you want to employ the important strategy of giving them the benefit of the doubt as to their *motivation* when you ask them to be aware of and change the problematic behavior. You might say something such as, "I know you really don't like it when I get angry at you, but when you tease me, it would be easy for someone who does not know you so well to think that you really don't love me."

ACKNOWLEDGE THAT THE CONVERSATION IS HARD FOR THEM

When your parent has a hard time discussing a certain topic, say, "I know this is hard to talk about, but it sounds like it is something we really need to face."

ASSUME THEIR INTELLIGENCE

When you wish to bring up for discussion the obvious ways in which your parent's repetitive behaviors create problems, without insulting his or her intelligence, try this handy phrase: "As I'm sure you already know, nagging me does not seem to accomplish anything."

CLARIFY YOUR INTENTIONS

If you are trying to discuss problematic behavior coming from other relatives in the past or present, and your parent defends them despite being furious with them for the same behavior you are bringing up, this may impede a useful and empathic discussion about the possible reasons for that family member's misbehavior. A useful disclaimer that may prevent this from happening is, "I'm not trying to turn [relative] into a villain, but..."

5. Playing Stupid

Asking anyone about their motives for their engaging in a particular course of action can be a tricky proposition. Merely asking, "Why did you do that?" can sound like a barely concealed accusation of wrongdoing, akin to asking a child, "Why is your hand in the cookie jar?" This can be especially problematic if you are asking your parents about behavior you obviously do not like, such as ICDD responses. Furthermore, when your parents are ambivalent about their own behavior and also feel that they need to conceal their real motives because they are trying to follow a family rule, getting answers becomes even more difficult. They may also feel ashamed of their inability or unwillingness to challenge those rules.

Under these circumstances, yet another way your parents may avoid clearly describing their motives is by playing stupid. They may claim they have no idea why they had this, that, or the other ICDD reaction. In such cases, "I don't know" is usually code for "I don't want to think about it," "I'm not going to tell you," or both.

Countermove: *Suggest They Have a Good Reason*

An alternative to asking a "Why do you do that?" question is saying, "You must really have a good reason for doing X. You can obviously see the [specified problems] it creates for both of us, and I don't think you're really happy about [the outcome]."

Use of the phrase "good reason" undercuts the sense of accusation inherent in "why" questions, as you are implying that the reason for their behavior is, at the very least, logical. Furthermore, this wording implies that they are doing what they do *in spite* of the downside, rather than *intentionally creating* the downside. This is much more empathic than other alternative ways to ask the reasons for someone's behavior.

Even so, your parents may not respond by either thinking more about their own motives or by telling you about them. They may just shrug their shoulders or otherwise express their resistance or indifference. However, they may also start to think more about the issues you raised, which increases the chances of having an even more fruitful conversation later on.

They also may start talking about not doing whatever it was that bothers you. While not as complete a response as their discussing the connection between their real motives and the family history and the family rules, it is nonetheless a good outcome if they stick to their promises. If they do not, you have set the stage for posing the question a second time.

6. Shifting the Blame to You

One trick that a family member targeted for metacommunication can use to get you to back off is to suddenly bring up *your* behavior, with a sort of a "Well, *you're* one to talk" attitude. They may try to shift the blame at least partially back onto you by bringing up your contribution to any difficult interactions. They expect you to respond either overtly, by backing off from trying to metacommunicate, or indirectly, by engaging with them in some sort of unwinnable argument.

Countermove: *Freely Acknowledge Your Contribution*

As described in chapter 2, you have been contributing to the problem yourself all along—usually by trying to placate them by doing whatever it was that they seemed to need from you. To keep the metacommunication process going, however, you can explain in a very matter-of-fact and quiet way that your behavior was based on your *reaction* to your parent's repetitive behavior.

Oliver's parents complained that he was a terrible financial burden to them, even though they always compulsively took care of his every financial need, whether he seemed to need them to or not. In fact, they usually gave him way more money than he really wanted or asked for. During an attempt to discuss the family dynamics, at first he strategically did not bring up the double message he had been getting, but instead expressed empathy for all the financial problems his parents were having as they neared retirement.

"Well, you certainly don't seem to have any trouble taking all the money we give you!" his mother predictably shot back. He replied, "Yes, I certainly have taken the money. That is because you always seem so disappointed when I don't."

You can phrase this as a disclaimer to stop counterproductive arguments over who exactly is to blame for a given repetitive problematic interaction. You might say, "I certainly contributed to this, and I think neither of us is happy with it continuing. I wonder if we lock horns because both of us were taught growing up that [your family myth], but we are not comfortable with it."

7. Changing the Subject

A simple maneuver for avoiding a topic of conversation is simply to change the subject. There are a variety of ways to accomplish this feat. Going off on a tangent is a big one—it warrants its own section, so it will be discussed separately. Subject changes may be accomplished either somewhat abruptly or insidiously, such as by using a break in the conversation to bring up an unrelated subject, knowing that the new subject interests the other person. Your parent may make jokes about a shared mutual experience, or look for something in the immediate environment that can be used as a distraction, as in, "Do you see what the cat is doing? Look, over there!"

Countermove: *Politely Point Out the Change and Go Back to the Original Subject*

The first rule in dealing with subject changes of this sort is to be on the lookout for them so you know when they have occurred. Often when two people are engrossed in an engaging conversation, the original subject will simply be glossed over or seemingly forgotten. When you notice a subject switch, attempt to bring the conversation right back to the previous subject. If that fails, you can then point out the subject change by casually mentioning—in a nonjudgmental manner—that there has been a change, and expressing a desire to get back to the original issue.

If your parents persist in sidetracking maneuvers, you can handle this in the same way you handle any defensive reaction. Step back and ask yourself why the target is becoming uncomfortable. Then either attempt to empathize by looking for a reasonable motive behind their changing the subject, or express puzzlement over the target's reluctance to address your concerns.

8. Going off on a Tangent

A trick frequently used to derail metacommunication is to mix several separate but highly interconnected issues, moving from one to the other in a way that leads to an outcome in which none of them get covered to the point where alternatives can be discussed. This prevents conflict resolution. Family rules about which behaviors are expected, allowed, or disallowed over a given issue often involve several different aspects of behavior, as well as differing—or even contradictory—expectations in different social contexts. Family members may be conflicted about some of these rules, but not others. However, when it comes to any given cultural issue, these various aspects and expectations tend to all be interrelated and intertwine with one another.

For example, when strict religious mandates are the issue, a genogram might reveal several issues: whether people in the family should ever be proud of their accomplishments or should instead give all the credit to God, whether it is admissible to stand out from a crowd, whether one can challenge the theology of the church hierarchy or advocate changes based on what one knows from other sources or other denominations, what it means to side with one faction within church politics over another, and whether one can socialize with people outside the church or should shun such contact. Because these aspects are all so interconnected, it is indeed difficult to talk about any one of them without talking about the others.

Caleb's father Jeremiah had strong theological ambivalence about taking personal pride in things and about being prideful in general. Jeremiah preached going along with the mandates of moral behavior as dictated by the pastor of their church, and he spoke out against any individuals who seemed to be pridefully thinking they were superior because they knew better. On the other hand, he seemed unhappy about many church teachings and frequently challenged the pastor on the interpretation of scripture. The latter activity fueled contentious church politics among members of their congregation, who would often feel the need to take sides. However, when Caleb challenged some church doctrine, just as his father did, Jeremiah seemed to become unstable and grow verbally abusive.

Whenever Caleb brought up his confusion about this state of affairs, Jeremiah would begin expounding about various theological debates among assorted factions within the church, concerning a wide variety of subjects. Conversations led to tangents about some theological question, and no resolution of the underlying dilemma seemed possible.

Since we know that family dysfunction has its roots in ambivalence over various family rules and prohibitions, anything Jeremiah said to his son regarding these issues can be roughly translated into a message to the son to either "act (or relate to the church) like me" or its polar opposite, "do not act (or relate to the church) like me." Often both within the very same conversation or even the same sentence! Because of Jeremiah's ambivalence over his family rules regarding church activities, Caleb could not really know which of these two messages his father was trying to send at any given time.

I have frequently observed families that bring up a number of tangential issues, one by one in sequence, with the discussion of each one subtly morphing into being about the next one, and so forth, until the conversation eventually returns to the original issue. Then the whole circle starts all over again! They talk in circles.

Countermove: *Stick with the Core CCRT Theme*

Each tangent starts from the same core theme. When you think of it this way, you can use the tangent's connection to the core theme to return to it. Metacommunicators can use the tangent as *just another example* of the very problem they are trying to solve.

As a strategy for countering the tangent issue, Caleb expressed confusion about what his father was trying to tell him. He found he could do this *no matter which theological debate was brought up.* Caleb started by saying, "Dad, sometimes it sounds like you are criticizing me for doing the same things you do, while at other times it sounds like you are criticizing me for *not* doing them. I'm confused about what you think is the right strategy when a big disagreement breaks out between our pastor and various factions in the congregation. And if I do take sides, am I not acting all self-important?"

Rather than addressing the question of whether Caleb should or should not emulate his behavior, Jeremiah tried to go off on a tangent by giving advice. The conversation went like this:

Dad: It is probably best not to take sides.

Son: But don't you keep doing that?

Dad: Well, I do that because the pastor himself is acting prideful, like he is superior to everyone.

Son: But doesn't making that judgment mean that you have superior knowledge about what is theologically correct? Doesn't that make you seem overly prideful?

Dad: Have you been hanging out with that atheist friend of yours again?

The last question changes the subject from what it means to get involved in theological debates within the church to a criticism of the son for being influenced by people outside their denomination. Without a countermove, tangents like this would prevent father and son from ever (1) clearly addressing the underlying ambivalence they both feel about some of the church orthodoxy and (2) possibly resolving that ambivalence.

If Caleb had used this countermove—taking each tangent Jeremiah goes off on, and using it as another example of the original issue—any criticism the father made of the son on any of these interrelated subjects could have been framed as causing the exact same confusion as the last one created. Instead of saying, "Doesn't that make you seem overly prideful?" Caleb could have said, "I'm confused when you say that, because it sounds like you are saying that sometimes people do have better ideas about these matters than other people do."

And when Jeremiah suddenly brought up the criticism about mixing with outsiders, Caleb would have been ill-advised to come right out and accuse his father of being inconsistent or even hypo-critical, as that would lead him to becoming defensive. The tangent would continue if Caleb said, for example, "But doing that is itself is a matter of debate in the church! They think we need to do that in order to proselytize."

With the recommended countermove, Caleb would also blame any misunderstanding on his *own* confusion about what Jeremiah is trying to say: "I just don't get it, Dad. Does taking a stand on issues such as these open a person up to the accusation that he is not acting humble in the eyes of the Lord? Or is it important to stand up for what he feels is right?"

9. Nitpicking and Overgeneralizing Your Examples

This defense is marshaled during discussions of problematic parental behavior in which you need to bring up specific examples in order to make a point. A big problem with the use of any example is that, no matter how clear-cut an illustration of a problem it may appear to be, aspects of it will always be open to nuances of interpretation. A parent can often sidetrack an attempt at metacommunication by quibbling with some minor detail in any example you might bring up, in a way that invalidates your whole point about how problem-atic the interactions are.

Or, instead of nitpicking, a parent may take a seemingly oppo-site tack to nitpicking to achieve the same purpose: they may accuse you of overgeneralizing. After all, no matter how often individuals behave in a similar fashion, there are always going to be times when they do not act that way. In fact, they may at times do the exact opposite. Recall that ambivalence over family rules creates contradictory behavior, which frequently creates a confusing mixed message. A hateful person is sometimes loving, an incompetent one is sometimes competent, and so on. Your parent may back up their overgeneralizing accusation about their hateful or incompetent behavior with examples of the infrequent times when they had been loving or competent.

Judy has been acting like a surrogate parent for her own mother. She attempts to discuss her reactions to the mother's frequent and unreasonable requests for immediate assistance. If Judy brings up a recent example, her mother easily confuses the issue by quibbling over the reasonableness of her request for assistance in that particular instance, while completely ignoring all of the other instances— not to mention their frequency. After all, the urgency of a need for assistance is always open to debate. The attempt at metacommunication might then turn into an unwinnable argument over how badly the mother needed help on one particular night a few weeks ago. The issue of the effect of the mother's *overall* behavior on her daughter would be entirely lost. If you are alert to these maneuvers, you can try the following countermoves so that you do not get embroiled in sidetracked arguments over trivial issues.

Countermove: *Validate Kernels of Truth*

To counter nitpicking, a useful and empathic response is to validate the kernel of truth in your parent's protestation: "Well, you are right; that may not be a perfect example of what I'm talking about, *but*" (said firmly) "there are many instances when this sort of thing happens. I think you know what I'm talking about." You might also bring up the fact that there has been a whole series of interactions that, while all different to some degree, seem to follow a similar overall pattern. You can then make the overall pattern the topic of the conversation, while refusing to argue about whether any specific example is truly representative. (We will discuss the *kernel of truth* strategy further, later in this chapter.)

Do not get dragged into an unwinnable argument over the validity of your opinions about what happened during any one specific incident, or what the example might mean for your relationship with your parent. If you already know that your parent is prone to nitpick, and especially if you have already brought up examples of a problem in prior conversations, you can say, "I've already given you examples, so there's no point in my doing that again; I think you know what I'm talking about." Then refuse to give any more examples.

The females in Kara's family seemed to be overly dependent on the males, but at the same time, their verbal comments indicated a marked disdain for males. Both Kara and her mother, Nicole, had cleaned up after their fair share of alcoholics. Nicole constantly spoke of how irresponsible the male of the species is, and how a woman is obligated to make sacrifices for her husbands and lovers. Such statements had a striking effect on Kara, who felt obliged to go along with Nicole's opinion of men by rejecting any potential suitor who might challenge that opinion by exhibiting real strength.

In the course of a discussion about the family problem, Nicole protested that Kara was overgeneralizing. While the mother had had several irresponsible partners, her current lover was very dependable—and Kara knew it. She quickly admitted that her mother's current relationship did seem to be an exception. However, she empathically added, "Nonetheless, in light of your horrible experiences with your own father and your previous husbands, I can see why you might be concerned about the inadequacies of men. I wanted you to know how your statements about this over the years have affected me."

When discussing the problematic behavior of any family member, you can sometimes avoid nitpicking accusations that you're ignoring counterexamples of times when a problematic interaction did *not* occur by steering clear of words such as "always" and "never." However, if you are called out about overgeneralizing, the counter-move is to agree that the counterexample is valid while still maintaining that *most of the time* the parent behaves as you have described. Additionally, in cases of mixed messages, you can productively use the counterexample to strengthen the very point that you are trying to make. The counterexample might indicate the presence of a conflict in the person being discussed, or might be evidence of some hidden quality that he or she possesses but wants to hide for some reason. In Kara's case, the fact that her mother's current boyfriend was dependable may mean Nicole had changed her thinking recently, which would be a valuable point of discussion for Kara.

10. Double Binds

You may have been placed in some sort of double bind by a parent repeatedly over many years. When it comes to certain decisions, they criticize you no matter which alternative course of action you choose. It's extremely annoying to be placed in this damned-if-you-do-and-damned-if-you-don't position. Over time it leads to feelings of frustration and helplessness, which in turn can lead to feelings of anger or unhappiness. To discuss the problem effectively with the goal of stopping or altering it, the double bind must at some point become the subject of metacommunication. Remaining empathic is, again, a difficult but necessary prerequisite for this strategy to be effective.

Your parents might even try to derail your attempt at metacommunication by putting you in yet another double bind, which may or may not be similar to the one that you have been attempting to discuss. Again, the key to remaining empathic is finding the good reason behind the parents' unreasonable behavior. Your parents have put you in a no-win situation because of their own internal conflict. They really feel it is *they* who cannot win.

Countermove: *Comment on the Bind*

The best countermove is for you to comment on the predicament your parent's behavior puts you in, and to use that as a way to draw a parallel to the confusion the parent must be experiencing about the issue. You can use the previously discussed strategies of expressing puzzlement over what the parents really expect of you. If you already have some idea why your parent is so conflicted over a particular course of action you chose, substitute a hypothesis about why the parent gets upset no matter how you choose. This hypothesis may be based on what you know about your family from your genogram.

This statement takes the following basic form: "When you do A, I get the feeling that you want me to do X, and when you do B, I get the feeling that you do *not* want me to do X. This is very confusing [irritating, and so on]. I am not sure what you want me to do. I wonder if you are confused about this yourself because of Y and Z." You can refer to the examples of Brianna and Tyler or Caleb and Jeremiah—both of which involve double binds.

11. Denial

"Denial" has become an interesting word. It used to mean that a person was stating, defensibly, that an allegation about his or her behavior is not true—but that no longer seems to be what the word means. It now almost seems to mean the exact opposite. With the spread of the 12-step approach to treating alcoholism, people who are said to be *in denial* are those who are supposedly avoiding facing facts about themselves that are actually true. When alcoholics are told that they cannot control their drinking, they often reply with, "I can stop drinking any time I want." The *denial* here means that such people really cannot control their drinking, but are denying this obvious fact, even to themselves.

I personally think that when alcoholics say this they are, in fact, telling the truth. They *can* stop drinking any time they want. Since they *do not* control their drinking much of the time, I think that what they are saying is that they are *unwilling* to do so, not that they are *unable* to do so. In fact, they do control their drinking all the time. Otherwise, they would all overdose soon after developing the addiction or end up in jail for public drunkenness each and every time a policeman happened by. While people clearly do lie to themselves as a defense mechanism, I think in many cases "deniers" are simply lying to other people to avoid telling them what is really going on. In metacommunication, this type of denial is used in the service of pretending that certain repetitive behavior patterns are a figment of the imagination of one of the parties—so that individual will shut up about it.

Using denial as an invalidating strategy, your parents tell you that something you are bringing up never happened. They tell you that you imagined it, that you have a faulty memory, or that you are just plain lying. Of course, in these situations, you know very well it did take place. Guess what? So do they! They, not you, are the ones being dishonest.

Consider, too, that you might succeed at getting past one level of their denial only to find they employ a second one against you. If you get past that one, a third one suddenly appears. And a fourth! Barrett and Trepper (1992) described the typical multiple layers of denial, which often come out one after another, in the same order each time. As you break through each layer of resistance, the next one pops up in its place. These multiple levels of denial are not, however, an excuse to avoid metacommunicating. Barrett and Trepper's predictable stages of denial are as follows, in order:

Denial of facts ("It never happened; you're a liar!")

Denial of awareness ("I was drunk" or "I didn't realize I was insulting you; you should have told me")

Denial of responsibility ("You were the one who attacked *me*; anyone would have responded that way")

Denial of impact ("It's only happened a few times" or "It's over; why do you always have to dwell on the past? You're just too sensitive; get over it!")

Countermove: *Kindly But Firmly Refuse to Argue About Past Events*

To counter your parent's denial of facts, open with a disclaimer, and then refuse to argue about the obvious. A kind but firm tone here is, as always, essential. This statement takes the form, "Look, Dad, my goal is not to make you eat crow about this or even to make you feel bad, but you and I both know what has been happening, so there's no use in pretending otherwise. Not talking about this just makes us walk on eggshells around each other, and I know you are as uncomfortable about that as I am."

If your parent goes on to deny awareness or responsibility, do not get into an argument. Proceed, without actually saying what you are doing, as if you and your parent both know the denials are meant to avoid the issue. Again, start with a disclaimer: "I know this is hard to talk about, Dad. It is hard for me to bring it up too. But it's not like this has just happened once; it keeps happening over and over. We need to get this subject on the table so we can have a better relationship."

With his denial of impact, again, just refuse to argue. If you are told you are making too big a deal over something trivial or that you are oversensitive, you can say, "That could be, but it really bothers me, and I'm sure you really don't want to have that effect on me."

Countermove: *Stick to Your Point*

Deniers frequently go on to quibble about the *details* of the alleged incidents. Denial can morph into nitpicking. Nobody can remember every detail of a past encounter. You may not remember exactly when an incident took place or the color of your parent's shirt, but you are highly unlikely to get an incident of significant mistreatment mixed up with a fun trip to a football game. When confronted with quibbling about a detail in order to invalidate your memory, your next move is to bring the conversation back to the original point you were trying to make, as in, "We can argue about the details forever, but they're kinda irrelevant. We both know what's important here."

12. Counteraccusations

A favorite maneuver used by many parents to scuttle metacommunication is the counteraccusation. Whenever you attempt to discuss a mutual problem with your parent without placing blame on anyone, you may need to bring up examples of her behavior that you find troublesome. Even when you do your best not to blame, even admitting that you yourself have done many of the things for which you may criticize others, your parent may still become indignant. Rather than lying about her behavior, she might instead place the blame for the problem *entirely* on you, or she might also try to infuriate you by grossly exaggerating your contribution to the problem. Doing so is invalidating to you, to say the least, because it transforms what you perceive as your parent's offensive behavior into something you have done that offends her.

When this happens, you will be sorely tempted to return the insult in kind. As with any other distancing maneuver, however, you should instead react by using the counteraccusation as a means to move closer to your parent and to help the conversation proceed rather than come to an abrupt end.

Countermove: *The Kernel of Truth*

There will invariably be at least a *kernel of truth* in the counteraccusation, no matter how overblown it is. As discussed in chapter 2 and elsewhere, since you are an integral part of the family system, you are indeed part of the problem. If you react to the accusation by merely defending yourself, your parents will have a wealth of examples from your past as ammunition to back up their charge—and they'll use them. You may start feeling frustrated or guilty about your contributions to the family problem, and the conversation will be sidetracked. However, you can use the kernel of truth in their accusation to get the conversation back on track. You can use it in the service of empathy.

Look for the kernel of truth in their attack, and agree with that—and only that. *Simply ignore* all the nastiness, exaggerations, and negative implications of the targeted family member's comments. After acknowledging the kernel of truth in their accusation, use your admitted contribution to the problem as an example of behavior that is caused by the very parent-child problem you are now trying to discuss and solve. In turn, this will allow you to ask how *together* you can change the problematic relationship pattern for the better.

You can also use the counteraccusation to question traditional family beliefs. Wayne, who had been estranged from his family and living far away, finally decided to take the bull by the horns and call his father, Phil, to metacommunicate about the family problem. He let Phil know that he wanted to come home on vacation to clarify some of the family issues. Phil immediately began to indignantly criticize Wayne's attempt at renewed family involvement. "You moved away and have your own life. Who are you to come back here and try to fix the family?" This apparent criticism was covertly a "distancing" remark—seemingly expressing a negative attitude. But in reality, it was a covert code for the altruistic sentiment, "You are better off being two thousand miles away from us."

Wayne responded, "I can understand your feelings. I often asked myself that same question when I first considered doing this. I have been away a long time, and I'm just not happy about not being close to the family." His goal was to bring up the difficulty that the entire family faced: being enmeshed with one another but unhappy about it. Their dilemma was how to remain close to one another while still leading somewhat independent lives.

Before Wayne could follow that intention, however, Phil made an exaggerated counteraccusation. "Look," Phil protested, "forget it. You're just going to stir up trouble. We are not going to change. Your mother has been binge drinking for years, and she isn't going to stop. You're not going to save anyone." This was an admission of the family myth that people cannot change their basic nature. The accusation that Wayne was trying to be the family savior, and that this was a major cause of trouble, was particularly bothersome to Wayne. In the distant past he had, in truth, made valiant attempts to get his mother to stop drinking. But he stopped doing so after attending Al-Anon, an organization that helps family members of alcoholics. The futility of trying to save an alcoholic from herself is one of the hallmarks of their message to "Let go and let God." Phil knew this, but seemed to be completely discounting Wayne's effort to relinquish the job of trying to save his mother.

Wayne bit his tongue; then he said, "Yeah, I already know that. But avoiding everyone is not helping matters either, and I don't want to just keep doing that." He hoped this comment would set the foundation for future negotiations with his father that would allow them to establish new rules for a better relationship.

A common counteraccusation is the statement, "You don't really care about me. You're just trying to [set me up, make yourself look like the good guy, and so forth]." You cannot "win" this sort of argument, because no one can read minds, so there's no way to prove whether or not you care about anything. So *do not bother* talking about it. Reply with something like "I wish I could prove to you that that is not the case," then merely refuse to elaborate or argue the point any further.

Another counteraccusation merely *sounds* like a negative personal insult, but reflects an ambiguity: "I cannot *believe* that you would talk to me like this!" You can respond, "Yeah, I can hardly believe I'm bringing this up myself, but I think it's really important!"

13. The Mea Culpa Response

Sometimes, instead of going into denial mode when confronted over their problematic behavior, parents may do what seems to be the exact opposite. Mom might suddenly break into tears, apologize profusely, and then go on and on about what an awful mother she has been—or even about what an awful person she is in general. This is invalidating you, as it is designed to cut off your complaint and reframe your attempt at metacommunication into your having maliciously made your parents feel bad for their shortcomings.

Sometimes *mea culpa* rants sound either like manipulative guilt trips or completely phony, in which case you may have the understandable urge to respond with a snide or sarcastic response, like, "Oh, yeah? Like you *really* feel bad about that." But they may also sound quite genuine. You may not believe they are ever genuine, because your parent's behaviors blatantly contradict them. But usually the guilty feelings your parent has expressed have a real basis. Your parent is too afraid to clearly and unequivocally admit to these feelings, so she exaggerates them and uses them against you.

Rather than becoming sarcastic, an opposite urge may kick in for you: to protect your parent. You may start to feel sorry for her, and therefore reassure her that she is not really all that awful, or even start to say that her misbehavior is really not so bad after all. Unfortunately, this will scuttle any effort at discussing the family processes, so resist this urge.

Countermove: *Ignore Guilt Trips*

Your parents' guilt-trippy tone in a mea culpa response is meant to make you question whether they really do, or do not, feel bad. I recommend that you just *assume* they do feel bad, and basically ignore the ambiguous aspect of what they say. Then apply the next countermove.

Countermove: *Let Them Feel It*

It is okay for your parents to feel bad about what they have done. In fact, they already do, and in the short run you really cannot save them from that anyway. So let them feel what they feel. They can take it. If they start to cry (and you are with them, not on the phone with them), do what therapists do: hand them a box of tissues.

Countermove: *Express Puzzlement Over the Double Message*

Next, express puzzlement over what is motivating your parent, incorporating a question about the double message she is giving to you. You might say, "Mom, I can really see that you feel bad about this. So it's even more confusing to me why it is that you *keep doing it anyway.*"

14. Fatalism

Fatalism is the belief that all events are predetermined and therefore inevitable, so there is nothing anyone can really do about them. Therefore, why even try? Fatalists believe that people are essentially helpless. A sense of fatalism is a characteristic of the belief systems of some cultural groups; if your parents or their forebears have this heritage, it may endure among the family rules.

Fatalism can show up as accusations that you are being a troublemaker. Alternatively, you might be accused of trying to act like a therapist with no qualifications: "Quit trying to analyze everything!" is a frequent family rallying cry. Or you may be told that you are a sadist who is trying to open old wounds: "Why are you bringing this up? It's all in the past."

Even though expressing fatalistic beliefs may not seem to be a major form of invalidation, and countering it is often fairly straightforward, it is nonetheless a biggie. None of the other invalidating maneuvers discussed so far questions even the possibility of solving ICDD problems to the extent that fatalistic defenses do.

Instead of reacting negatively by withdrawing or attacking in response to these types of statements, you can use them as an entry point to question fatalistic family belief systems. You can probably empathize with the family fatalism by thinking about times in which your prior attempts at problem solving with your family failed miserably, and you felt hopeless about ever changing the patterns.

Countermove: *Share the Concern but Question the Belief*

If you have ever felt hopeless about fixing things in your family relationships—and if your family is fatalistic, then you probably have—I recommend that you respond by admitting to them that you used to think just as they do, but add that you now have real doubts about those ideas.

"Why *shouldn't* we try to analyze the situation?" you may ask. "Understanding a problem is essential for figuring out a way to solve it." You might also offer a hypothesis about why people might think they are stuck with the way things are. Your parents may feel helpless about changing their future because of experiences or catastrophes that befell their forebears, but, as you can point out, times have changed.

In response to the accusation that you are dwelling on the past, you can point out how those past situations are *still* affecting the present in negative ways, and that this does not have to continue. Alternatively, you can say that you are bringing up problems because you want to have better relationships with them. The old problems are creating friction and distance, and you want to be closer.

As for the charge that you are being a troublemaker and creating discomfort for family members, you can reply that the dissonance *already* exists and will continue to exist if you all don't discuss it. In fact, stopping the behavior patterns that continue to create discomfort in your parents is by far the best way to relieve them.

Fatalism is often combined with overgeneralizations to imply that anyone who tries to solve problems is wasting their time. An example is, "Everyone will exploit you if given half a chance; the world is nothing but a toilet bowl. You better just get used to it!" The problem here is that if you agree, you are collaborating in this hyperbole as well as saying negative things about another inhabitant of the toilet bowl: you. On the other hand, if you disagree, then you are accused of invalidating and putting the speaker down. In this situation, you need to again look for the kernel of truth in the parent's statement, validate it, ignore the hyperbole, and use it to illustrate or obtain more information about some family issue that can then be a jumping-off point for further metacommunication. You might casually reply, "Well, the world can really be a crappy place. That's for sure! It sounds like you must have been really mistreated in your life."

15. Continuing to Pick a Fight No Matter What You Say

None of the recommended countermeasures described in this book are guaranteed to work. In fact, despite your having remained cool, calm, and empathic, a parent may continue to escalate with more and more outrageous accusations, irrationality, or invalidation with your every effort to counter the previous version. In such cases, you can assume that he is picking a fight with you on purpose—entirely for the sake of avoiding an issue.

Countermove: *Call It Out*

You can respond by firmly inquiring, "Why are you picking a fight with me?" Once again, you should refuse to argue the obvious by debating him about whether or not he is indeed picking a fight. This question often forces him into a situation in which he must either stop the escalating behavior or explain why he wants to have a fight. Metacommunication will advance, either way. If instead he ignores you and continues to pick a fight, you may need to temporarily back off, as will be discussed at the end of this chapter.

16. An Abrupt Switch

Another ingenious maneuver you need to watch out for may come as quite a surprise. Right in the middle of a heated discussion, amid a series of invalidating or ambiguous responses, your parents may, without warning and when you least expect it, execute this big diversionary tactic: talking about the very parent-child issues you were trying to discuss with them in the first place. For example, they may be acting as if they are furious over some imagined slight you allegedly made, but then suddenly seem to forget all about it and begin to talk about family dynamics—as if the feelings about you they had just expressed had never even come up.

When they do this, you may be induced to derail the metacommunication effort yourself! Their sudden dropping of an argument will leave you with a feeling that something is unfinished, even though at some level you know it was just a big diversion in the first place. The natural urge for most people is to get right back into the abandoned argument. The feeling created by the sudden switch is analogous to what you may have experienced in trying to get talkative friends off the phone when you have something else you must do. You tell them you have to get off, but they keep on talking, until you get flustered and insist in an annoyed tone that you *have* to go. They then respond with a sudden, angry, "Okay, goodbye!" Your natural, automatic response may be, "Wait! Don't hang up!" (Translation: "Don't go away *mad*.") Getting them off the phone, however, had been your goal in the first place.

Countermove: *Go Along With the Switch*

If you are able to catch on to this tactic in time, pretend—just as they are doing—that the big argument never even happened.

After all, that "fight" was nothing but a big red herring in the first place. They have now switched to problem-solving mode. Good! Be glad.

17. Walking Out

Parents commonly end an uncomfortable conversation with "I'm not going to talk about this," followed by their exiting the room or perhaps even covering their ears as a small child might. When your parent does this, it's usually not a good idea to immediately follow her as she sashays into the next room, as that usually only leads to further angry huffing and puffing.

Countermove: *Bring It up at the Next Opportune Time*

You want to demonstrate to your parent that her reluctance to talk about an issue will not make you give up trying to discuss it. On the other hand, you are not going to try to bully her into doing it. After things have calmed down, and as soon as an opportunity presents itself, empathically say something to the effect of, "I realize when I raise the subject of [whatever it was], it is very hard for you to talk about. It's hard for me too. I suspect that you are not happy with things as they have been, either, and I want us to have a better relationship. Don't you think we need to clear the air?"

EXERCISE: Which Responses Do My Parents Use?

At the beginning of the section on anticipating parental defensive reactions, I asked you to notice, as you went through them, which ones ring a bell for you or bring up memories of similar interactions from your past. Now that you have finished reading all of them, go back and peruse the categories again. Make predictions about which of them you think you may be likely to encounter in your own family. Although we have not yet discussed different strategies for initiating the whole process of metacommunication, it is not too early to start thinking about this. You should also think about your family history, and about CCRT themes or experiences from their own upbringing that are likely to make them feel the need to employ defenses against your efforts to metacommunicate about ICDD interactions.

You can also start identifying which of the various listed countermoves are most likely to be successful with each of your parents. Remember, you have been living with them your whole life, or most of it, and you are probably better than you think at predicting their responses. If you think about one of the countermoves listed and have no idea what your parents might say in response, that often means that they may be stymied by your intervention as well. That can be a good thing. In such cases, they may very well be at a loss for devising another move to get you off track. This may force them to start thinking less reactively about the issues in question.

Last, as part of this exercise, start practicing delivering some of the countermoves you have chosen in front of a mirror or, better yet, record yourself doing this. Practice makes it more likely that you will be able to stick to the script you have in mind when the time comes to confront your parents. In the next chapter, we will also discuss recruiting a significant other to help you practice.

You have now learned about possible ways your parents may behave if they are highly conflicted about their own behavior and give you mixed, ICDD messages about what they expect from you, as well as some effective countermeasures you can take to turn a dysfunctional interaction into an effective problem-solving session.

Before you can get started with confronting your parents, however, consider one more possible complication: the reactions that you may get from other important family members. In particular, we need to first discuss how significant others can themselves be part of the family problem, ways they may try to interfere with your efforts, and how best to prevent that.

CHAPTER 7

Bring Significant Others and Siblings on Board

Other people may be involved with perpetuating your parents' problematic behavior for many of the same reasons that you may be feeding into them—doing so in order to stabilize family homeostasis. You may need to deal with these people first, to clear the ground for a confrontation with your parents. This chapter will look at why and how your significant other (SO) and siblings (or other close relatives like aunts and uncles) may be playing a role in perpetuating the current dysfunction with your parents. It will discuss why they might try to sabotage your efforts to deal with your parents' ICDD behavior and how you can prevent that, or at least minimize any potential damage they might do.

Your relationships with romantic partners are of course quite different from your relationships with close relatives. While your SO may be your life partner, siblings are generally more peripheral to your everyday life. Even so, in order to confront a parent, you may need to try to minimize any potential interference from them. Getting someone out of the middle of a conflicted relationship between any two other people is referred to as "detriangulation."

With an SO, in some cases you can use the same detriangulation strategies that I will describe when we get to a discussion of siblings. However, it is often more useful to try to recruit an SO as an ally in your efforts rather than merely stopping the SO from being an impediment. The challenge is that your changing the relationship with your own parents may have severe, negative consequences for the relationship between your SO and *his or her* parents.

Why SOs Can Feel Threatened

When you are constantly trying to stabilize your unstable parents, you usually have to suppress aspects of yourself. This is difficult. In such cases, you are highly likely to pick an SO who has chosen to help you in your efforts. Helping one another out in maintaining homeostasis in respective families of origin often helps forge a deeper bond between romantic partners early on in their relationship.

People with problematic parents often pick mates whose relationships with their own parents involve the same CCRTs. Their respective family problems either mirror or dovetail with each other. In fact, each member of the couple often volunteers to "help" or "enable" the other to continue to stabilize their respective parents. This "I'll enable you if you'll enable me" dynamic is also called a "marital quid pro quo" or "mutual role function support." It is a more generalized version of the process of codependency described in the literature on families and couples with alcohol or drug issues.

I have found, over years of doing family-oriented psychotherapy, that SOs are frequently experts on their in-laws. They sometimes know things about them that their own SO, the child of those in-laws, does not know. They have keenly observed the troublesome interactions between their SOs and their in-laws; they have opinions about the reasons behind them, and they worry about what might happen if their SO attempts to alter those interactions. They are well aware that some of their SO's problematic behavior in other contexts—particularly within the romantic relationship itself—stems from their family dynamics.

Because couples share intrapsychic conflicts over the same CCRTs, the very things that attract them to one another in the first place may suddenly become major irritants in their marriage. The resulting friction is often their reason for seeking marital counseling. Nonetheless, I've also learned that both partners will purposely *feed into* the very behavior that they are complaining about. Even worse, they are afraid to stop doing so.

Familiar Family Rules Are Attractive

So why and how does this pattern develop? The answer is found in the idea of "familiar discomfort." The family environment in which you were brought up is very familiar to you. Human beings naturally feel more comfortable dealing with the familiar than with the unfamiliar, even when they find many aspects of the familiar environment quite stressful or unpleasant. Familiar discomfort is, for most people, less anxiety-provoking than unfamiliar comfort! In familiar territory, we know the rules we should follow and the roles we need to play, and we do not have to make decisions that could lead to totally unintended—and even more undesirable—consequences.

Thus, people who come from families that are ambivalent about certain of their rules, desires, and impulses often are attracted to romantic partners who react in familiar ways because they come from families with similar issues. Furthermore, such a partner can be very knowledgeable about how to help someone who is experiencing ambivalence about family dynamics maintain a difficult homeostatic role. Here are some examples of how this can play out.

Two families can have, in common, conflicts over speaking up when angry that are expressed in different ways. In one family, the expression of any angry feelings may be met with swift and strong invalidating responses, leading individuals to develop what I describe as "emotional constipation." On the other hand, in another family with the same conflict, everyone responds by yelling back and swearing like drunken sailors. A person from the first family type will marry a person from family type number two, because their angry spouse helps them to partially express their pent-up anger. This helps the inhibited person, in keeping with his or her family's demands, to keep a lid on it when around them. Later on, the couple may seem to switch positions with each other: the wife from the boisterous family clams up, and the inhibited husband starts to express all the anger he has been storing up for years. But rarely are they both expressive or both inhibited at the same time.

In families with conflicts over how involved parents and adult children should be with one another, the parents may do various things to annoy their adult child, but then complain when that child stays away from them in response. If you fall into this category, your spouse may volunteer to play the role of a villain who is dominating you and stopping you from seeing them. This may be done surreptitiously, or blatantly, such as yelling out to you sarcastically, "Honey, your *mommy's* calling you" whenever she phones. Since your parents probably think that you are easily manipulated to begin with, they fall for it. This way, your family gets angry at your SO and not at you. Your SO is protecting you in that sense. Stepmothers may also volunteer to do something analogous for a father who is supposed to remain somewhat estranged from children from a first marriage. That role is the basis for the stereotype of the "wicked stepmother."

It sometimes seems as if potential romantic partners whose families are conflicted over the same impulses and ideas have an uncanny ability to find one another—almost as if they had some form of mental telepathy. They appear to be at opposite sides of a room full of people at a party and yet gravitate toward each other, soon leaving the party together to go off to do some partying of their own. I can't explain it.

The Tensions That Result From Change

When both members of a couple use one another in a codependent way, each person in the couple tends to secretly think that it is primarily the *other* person who wants and needs the relationship to *continue in its current form.* Why else would they engage in behaviors that keep it going?

So what makes this important in regard to your confronting your parents? If you are married, or seriously involved with a romantic partner, when you start to follow the recommendations in this book to address your issues with your parents, your partner may react very negatively. Since up to that point you seemed to need your partner to support the way in which you *had* previously been dealing with your parents, and your behavior has helped your partner in an analogous fashion, when you start to change, your partner might feel betrayed, for three reasons.

First, your partner may have been sacrificing some of his or her own needs to enable you. Now you are implying that your partner has been, in a sense, foolish for having done so. Your partner gave up important things for you, and now you seem to be saying that was really unnecessary. So were all those sacrifices really just pointless? In the case of a spouse who has played the role of villain keeping you from your family, you are in effect saying it wasn't necessary to take all that bad blood from your family. Can you blame your spouse for getting upset with you?

Second, your partner may realize that the enabling you have provided to deal with *the partner's* parents may no longer be forthcoming. However, your partner still needs it! Marital tension will likely rise steeply, creating a major distraction for you from the task of confronting your parents' ICDD behavior.

Third, your spouse may have witnessed the failure of your previous efforts at confronting your parents over their troublesome behavior, and may understandably worry that the same things will happen again. And guess who will be around to have to pick up the pieces of your broken soul after that occurs for the umpteenth time? Rather than helping you with the strategies this book will teach you, your spouse may very well—quite understandably—do whatever is necessary to discourage your efforts.

Isabel's Story: Original Agreements Betrayed

When Isabel married Bruce, she agreed to do many things about which she was covertly unhappy, but that she thought were important to him. She agreed to live in a house in the same neighborhood as his family, in a town she did not particularly like, and to join his family's church rather than one of her own denomination. She also dressed in a somewhat frumpy manner because Bruce seemed insecure about having an attractive wife. His parents frequently warned him to keep an eye on his wife because she was so attractive; they "joked" about his less-attractive looks, suggesting that she might not remain satisfied with him.

The "value" of a woman's helping her husband by soothing his ego had been preached to Isabel by her mother. As Isabel described her, her mother seemed to be a firm believer that most men are really insecure and weak.

After going through psychotherapy, Bruce began to speak up to his parents about their annoying insistence on his remaining in both their town and their church, as well as their constant warnings about his wife's attractiveness. He also began to talk about selling their house, moving to another city, and changing churches. Furthermore, he started to get on his wife's case for her frumpy way of dressing and for treating him like he had no self-confidence.

Despite all appearances to the contrary, all along, Bruce had been just as unhappy as Isabel with their original marital agreement. Even though he now wanted to change things in a direction Isabel had herself secretly desired, she suddenly started to become almost as critical of him as his parents had been previously. She complained to her own therapist that she had a strong feeling her husband had betrayed her, even though she could not explain to herself exactly why.

So, how can you more constructively handle the issues created by a relationship scenario such as this? How can you enlist your spouse as an ally in changing the way you deal with your parents?

Getting Your Partner on Board

You and your SO can alter your marital dynamics in productive ways as well as have a very fun and satisfying time by creating a "relationship about your relationship" (Wile 1981). You can devote part of your time together to working to stop enabling one another in playing roles for your respective families that neither of you really likes. The process of investigating the dynamics in your respective families of origin and seeing how your own relationship has been affected and shaped by them can be not only enlightening, but also a fascinating hobby you can enjoy together.

To proceed as I recommend requires a minimal level of good communication skills between you and your spouse. With some couples, these types of activities do not turn out well. In that case, you may need couples psychotherapy to help deal with your marital metacommunication skills—or lack thereof. Alternatively, each of you may need your own individual therapist who can help you to work on both your family-of-origin issues and your marital issues simultaneously. This will help you and your partner learn to assist one another in addressing family dynamics instead of fighting about them.

EXERCISE: Scripting a Discussion with Your SO

Write out a script for use with your SO for initiating and continuing a discussion about the issues just described. You will use this script to prepare yourself for the actual discussion. Of course, once you get started metacommunicating with your SO, you may come up against responses you were not prepared for or had not predicted. In that case, if you cannot keep a productive conversation on track, you always have the option of temporarily backing off and returning to the issue later, as described previously.

The conversation about family dynamics you will be planning, and then having, should follow this order:

1. Describe your own discoveries from this book and then describe your conclusions.

2. Ask what your SO has noticed about your family dynamics.

3. Let your SO know about your preliminary plans to confront your parents, and ask about any concerns about how that might turn out. If you have already started planning how you will approach your parents, you can let your SO know how you plan to address any concerns and stay safe (this is similar to part of the detriangulation strategy with siblings I'll describe shortly). If you have not yet reached that stage, you can still let your SO know that you will be taking serious potential problems—including your SO's concerns—into account as you plan your strategy.

4. Invite her to brainstorm about and discuss possible answers to questions about how your respective family dynamics may have affected your relationship. If you have never talked openly about this issue before, these questions may be more likely than others to lead to reactions from your SO that you have never seen before and did not predict in your script. Here are questions you can consider as you prepare:

    •   Did the family issues you discovered create any similar or analogous conflicts between the two of you? If so, in what ways?

    •   How might you be enabling each other because of parental reactions?

    •   Are the two of you perhaps misreading one another's motives because of your mutual obsession with playing dysfunctional family roles up to this point, and because it seems so difficult for you stop playing them? In other words, has your SO decided that you *really* want to keep playing a role because of that—and that you *really* want your SO to continue to support that role, even if you say you want to stop? (This problem frequently occurs when people try to change family rules—it's a phenomenon called the "game without end," which will be discussed further in the last chapter.) If so, how can you prevent this from happening?

- What might happen to your relationship if all of that were to change?

As you write out possible ways to phrase a conversation focused on these tasks, try to think of your SO's typical ways of responding when she becomes defensive—just as you did when thinking about your parents. What does she usually do when conversations start to get uncomfortable? Does your spouse, for example, become fatalistic or go off on tangents? As you write out your script, include a prediction about how your SO might thusly respond if you were to bring up a particular issue, as well as potential countermoves that you predict will work best for your SO in getting a conversation back on track. You can chose from any of the appropriate countermoves detailed in the previous chapters.

After having this discussion with your SO, you might also suggest that both of you read this book and share your reactions to it. Strongly consider asking your partner to work on his own genogram, just as you have constructed your own. Then, both of you can support one another's efforts to alter problematic reactions you receive from your parents as well as your respective in-laws.

You can be each other's "practice partners." Recruiting your spouse to role-play with you as you practice the strategies that you came up with after reading the previous chapter leads to even more effective practice than doing it by yourself in front of a mirror or with a recording device. Your partner probably knows your parents well and may also have a family that uses some of the same strategies for getting someone to be quiet that one of your parents uses. Therefore, she may be exceedingly accurate in portraying your parents in a role-play exercise. Not only that, but as she throws various defenses at you as she role-plays your parent, she can also give you direct feedback about whether you are sticking to your strategy and the tone of voice you are using. This is excellent practice for staying cool during the actual "combat" situation later on.

Sibling Involvement in Your Parents' Problematic Behavior Patterns

While you were learning ways to stabilize your parents when they were dealing with significant conflicts and ambivalence over family rules, any brothers and sisters you may have were dealing with these issues as well. While they may in some cases seem to be either uninvolved with your parent's ICDD behavior or far less of a target for it than you are, that is usually a result of the way your parents interacted with your siblings. As we shall see shortly, siblings may stay out of the way precisely because your parents focus their ambivalence more on you than on them.

In this section, I will describe three common ways your siblings may be involved with or feeding into your attempts to stabilize your parents.

Sibling Substitution

It should go without saying that parents do not treat all of their children in the same way. Even if they wanted to treat them all exactly alike, they could not, because each child has somewhat different genetic propensities and different experiences, which literally forces anyone else to respond to them differently. This issue can be particularly problematic in dysfunctional families, in which one sibling may bear the brunt of the parent's internal conflicts while all or some of the others may seem to escape relatively unscathed.

In dysfunctional families, generally at least one child is tagged "it" as the target of a parent's internal conflict over self-actualizing tendencies that break family rules. A child may be so tagged because of her position in the sibling birth order, whether it is the same as or the opposite of the parent's birth order, or because the child looks more like a problematic grandparent, or for any of several other possible reasons (Bowen 1978). The more dysfunctional the family is, the more additional children seem to be induced to develop problematic family-stabilizing functions. If for some reason the child tagged to be the primary family stabilizer suddenly reneges on the job and disappears, then another one of the children may feel obliged to step into that job. I refer to this as "sibling substitution."

You might feel guilty that if you do solve the problems you are having with a problematic parent, you could be sticking one of your siblings with the nasty job you had been doing. If so, as you proceed with the detriangulation strategies recommended in the next section, I suggest that you share what you know about the family genogram with a potential sibling substitute—much as you may have done with an SO. Of course, you should consider the ways in which your sibling might become defensive and plan how you might be able counter this. If the sibling will not listen and later steps into your role despite your efforts to help the sibling not to do so, that is the sibling's choice. It is not your responsibility to intervene any further.

Alexander's Story: Caretaking Sacrifices

Alexander came from a family that believed in a family myth that the first duty of adult children is to care for their aging parents, even if it means sacrificing their own marriages and careers. His family of origin was a sickly lot because of a genetic predisposition to two chronic illnesses. Of course, it is hard to get angry at sick parents in such a situation. It is not their fault they are sick. Nonetheless, taking care of them interfered with the lives of the adult children to a greater extent than most because of the family myth.

Alexander was the preferred caretaker for his ailing parents. He was the youngest family member and, following another family rule, remained unmarried so that he could fulfill this function. However, eventually he began to develop one of the genetic illnesses and was no longer capable of helping his parents as much. The family subsequently let him off the hook and turned to his older sister to fill the void. She was married, but after her parents turned to her, she suddenly began drinking too much. This ultimately led her husband to divorce her, leaving her with more time for her parent caretaking duties.

Sibling (or Sometimes Aunt or Uncle) Counselors

If you are the chosen one to fulfill some mandated role in your family, your unaffected siblings may seem to be very selfish when they pressure you to stay in a dysfunctional role, seemingly because it lets them off the hook. While they may be motivated in part by selfishness, keep in mind that they also feel pressure from the parents to do this because the parents are the ones who made the initial pick. The parent seems to strongly prefer the "it" sibling to handle the necessary tasks. The others fear the parent will react badly if one of the others does it instead.

Siblings may try to keep you in your place by sharing their "wisdom" with you, and telling you how your problems with Mom or Dad are entirely of your own making. Arguing with them about this is a waste of time. In such cases, you can just say there may be some truth to what they are saying and you are certainly willing to consider your own behavior, but proceed with the detriangulation strategy recommended in the next section.

Parents Stirring up Fights Between Siblings

In dysfunctional families, parents may create chronic and repetitive discord among the siblings through gossip. As first mentioned in chapter 3, this often happens when one sibling has been chosen to act out one side of the parent's intrapsychic conflict while the other acts out the other side. Again, think of a father who, conflicted over the value and necessity of hard work, may have one son who is a workaholic like him and another son who is a complete slacker. Rather than fight the conflict within himself, Dad vicariously watches as the two sons "fight it out."

The way sibling discord is engineered, the parents complain to sibling B about sibling A's behavior, behind A's back. They then turn around and complain to sibling A about sibling B's behavior, behind B's back. A and B get mad at each other on the basis of completely different views about what is going on between the other siblings and the parents.

If your attempts at stopping your sibling from interfering with your attempt to stop parental ICDD behavior (using the strategies I'll describe shortly) seem to be leading to arguments between you and the targeted sibling—arguments that are at best confusing and at worst infuriating—that's a strong indicator that such "sibling splitting" gossip is the cause. The remedy is straightforward: *share information* about the basis for your differing opinions, rather than just reacting to one another. You should stop arguing and ask your sibling, "Wait—what has Dad been telling you about me?" Then go on to share whatever Dad has been telling you about your sibling. Compare notes.

Detriangulation Strategy

In the chapter 1 discussion of family homeostasis, I mentioned that families have developed mechanisms for enforcing family rules whenever one member breaks them or even attempts to break them. Members of the family often gang up against offenders, telling them in so many words that they are wrong and they need to go back to following the old rules. They may say things like, "Who the hell do you think you are? You think you're so much better than us?" or "How can you treat your father that way?" I refer to this ganging-up tactic as "clustering."

If you try to metacommunicate with your parents about no-longer-adaptive family rules and their ambivalence about them, you are almost certainly breaking at least one of the rules right off the bat. Other peripheral family members—your siblings, aunts, and uncles—may become alarmed that your efforts will destabilize your parents, and they may come at you with a vengeance. Occasionally, more distant relatives step into the fray—sometimes even those who are not usually involved with your parents much at all.

Your other parent or one of your grandparents may also step in to protect a targeted parent; this is a somewhat different problem but can be resolved using a similar detriangulation strategy to this one. In huge families, it is sometimes useful to use this strategy with the patriarch or matriarch. The beneficial effects of this strategy may then percolate down to other potential triangulators.

If you use the detriangulation strategy I share in the following exercise with one parent—say, your father, in order to talk to your mother—it's likely your father will realize he is your next target. Surprisingly, if you use the recommended strategy, your father will nonetheless likely stay out of it. At some level, he too wants the family discord to cease. Once again, if you find that detriangulation strategies stir up an uncontrollable, frightening, and long-lasting hornet's nest instead of calming things down, hold off on the meta-communication effort until you can enlist the help of an appropriate therapist.

EXERCISE: Detriangulating Siblings and Relatives

Follow these steps to detriangulate relatives who may try to run interference for your parent.

1. **Inform the relative** about your plans to discuss certain problematic interactions you have identified (go ahead and name these) with your parent, and the changes that you plan to request.

2. **Ask the relative** what concerns he may have about the consequences of your plan. These concerns are generally similar to the concerns that may have come up for you while reading this book. Siblings and other relatives may fear that the parent will not be able to handle the confrontation and may begin to fall apart emotionally in some way. Or they may fear that the confrontation will create tensions in other important dyadic family relationships, such as between two parents, between a parent and a stepparent, or between

two generations—say, Mom and Grandpa. Even though you may have had the same fears, when another relative objects to your plan, it's still easy to become defensive about it or get angry with the person who objects. However, precisely because you have felt the same way, you can use that to create a very empathic response instead.

3. **Reassure the relative** that you have taken these concerns into account. If it is true, let the relative know that you have had similar concerns yourself but you have worked out a strategy that you believe will avoid any harm to anyone. Depending on whether the relative shows much interest or start getting curious, you can also talk about what you have learned about the family dynamics from the genogram, and what countermeasures to parental defensive reactions you think will solve the issues that concern this person.

4. **Stave off a power struggle,** as you end the conversation with a potential triangulator, by saying something like, "I really think it would be best if I handled this myself, so I would *really appreciate it* if you did not talk to Mom about this before I have a chance to. However, if you feel that you absolutely must alert her or talk to her about the issues as they apply to you, I'll understand."

Staving off a power struggle at the end of the detriangulation is perhaps the most important step, because you want to avoid such a struggle if at all possible. Your closing request often has a paradoxical effect on potential triangulators, and that is just what you want. It may induce them to stay clear of the whole endeavor when they otherwise may have been tempted to get involved. Siblings might say something like "Oh, no, you can do that one all by yourself. Leave me out of it!" They figure it's better that you take the heat than that they do.

On the other hand, because of familiar discomfort, they may still attempt to sabotage your efforts with your parents. If they take it on themselves to warn your parent or to interfere in some other way, you have given them your blessing. You will usually know if they have done so, sooner or later, and you can adjust your strategies with your parent accordingly—preferably without criticizing the person who has interfered.

Having cleared a pathway, you have now set the stage for the main event. At long last, it is time to consider how you will start metacommunication with the central players in your family drama, your parents.

PART THREE

HOW DO WE SHIFT TOWARD WARMTH AND ACCEPTANCE?

CHAPTER 8

Initiate Constructive Conversations

Despite any prior experiences that might make you pessimistic about your prospects, you *can* discuss family conflicts so that your parents can relate in positive ways. The skills described in this chapter will help you to start a constructive conversation with your parents that confronts ICDD patterns of behavior empathically and in a way that makes requests for change far more likely to succeed. If your understanding of the history of the family CCRTs from your research is partially or wholly incorrect, new information may emerge that will strengthen it and likely further clear up misunderstandings.

When metacommunicating, keep in mind that you want your parents to address, as dispassionately as possible, what has been happening. If they tend to deny the existence or the impact of important patterns, you need them to stop the denial. While a direct *admission* of wrongdoing on their part would be nice, it is not essential as long as they are discussing the patterns *as if* the patterns and your concerns about them are valid.

The first step is to find a way to meet with each person, one on one. Next, set up a time and place for your first conversation. Then choose an opening strategy from the five options I share and discuss later in this chapter (in "Strategies for Initiating the Conversation"). At least one of these will help you start to accomplish the following four goals with each person in your family:

- *Clarify your experience with each other.* You will be able to convey how you have been perceiving, or misperceiving, your parents' motives for problematic behaviors, so that your parents have a chance to correct any misinterpretations.

- *Look at the genogram together.* Although not absolutely necessary, generally it helps to share the understanding and knowledge that you gleaned from your genogram about the nature and the origins of the problematic family patterns, dilemmas, and conflicts under discussion.

- *Share the effect their behavior has on you.* When you let your parents know how their actions have affected you, if they do not wish to continue having that effect, the door is opened for change. Along the way, you may need to realistically debate the pros and cons of activities that challenge previously established family rules, as well as the value of being able to follow your own desires independently even when other family members may be uncomfortable with them for the reasons you clarified by investigating the family's history.

- *Open up the possibility for change.* The ultimate goal is requesting very concrete and specific changes to problematic behaviors and communication patterns. Most of the time, this will simply be for them to stop treating you in certain ways that trigger you and interfere with close family ties. After they agree to this, in principle, you can later begin to negotiate over what you all want your relationships to look like in the future. That is the topic of chapter 9.

After choosing your opening strategy, use the exercise that closes this chapter to help you think even further about, and anticipate, what might go wrong with the particular strategy you have picked before you actually proceed with it. If you have an SO or other individual who knows your family well, you can role-play the envisioned interaction to prepare yourself for any problems and to practice possible countermoves to anything that arises.

Plan to Meet, One to One

Each parent should be approached separately. Metacommunication works best with one person at a time. Trying to confront more than one parental figure at the same time is not a good idea, because the odds are good that they will gang up on you. Maintaining empathy is difficult enough when you are being invalidated by just one of them; trying to do so when being invalidated by clustering relatives is far more difficult.

Start by metacommunicating with the parent you think might be the most amenable, or the easiest to deal with. Then move on from that person to the more difficult ones, in order of difficulty. When you do this, if you experience some initial success in your efforts, you will generally be encouraged. This will make it much easier for you to persist if the going gets tougher.

Getting family members alone may involve a little strategy planning. Detriangulation efforts, as described in chapter 7, can clear the way for you to set up a meeting. But new problems can suddenly arise. Your target may get the idea that you are up to something, even if up to this point you have not said anything about what you plan to discuss. The target may, for example, have become suspicious when you asked about family history. If you have interviewed other relatives about genogram data, the others may have told your parents about your inquiries.

If your targeted parent seems to be resisting your efforts to have alone time with her, you can ask her straight out if the prospect of being with you is making her uncomfortable. If she denies it, it will be harder for her to continue to try to wiggle out of a meeting. If she admits to discomfort, be empathic with her fears while remaining persistent in requesting the meeting. Try a reassurance like "I promise I'm not going to try to beat you up about anything." If she seems to have an inkling about what you want to talk about, you can say something like, "I know certain topics are hard for both of us to discuss, but I think it's important that we address them."

Sometimes, one parent runs interference for the other by never seeming to allow the two of you to be together just by yourselves. With another parent hanging around all the time, you can respectfully ask permission to meet with the other one alone. Just say you would like to have some "alone time." If the other parent pushes you to explain why, tell the truth.

Setting a Time and Place

Setting up a specific "appointment" time with your parent reduces the chance that you will procrastinate over having the meeting, or that you will chicken out at the last moment.

Meeting your parent in person, face to face, is more likely to lead to a successful outcome than communicating over the phone or even via Skype. However, if your parent lives too far away and traveling is not possible, using the telephone or Skype is far better than not doing it at all.

I recommend meeting in neutral territory, if possible, rather than confronting parents at either your home or theirs. You want them to be comfortable, but not surrounded by reminders of their typical home situation in which they may have solidified their ICDD reactions. You might suggest taking them out to lunch at a quiet restaurant set up so that other diners are not likely to overhear the conversation. A public place has the added advantage of making it somewhat more difficult for those parents who are so inclined to yell in emotionally charged conversations or just get up and walk away. There is, however, no guarantee that they might not still do both, no matter where they are.

Strategies for Initiating the Conversation

Here are my five suggested strategies for initiating fruitful discussions with your parents or other attachment figures about their ICDD behavior. When you start to plan out your metacommunicative strategy, you will choose the one that seems least threatening to the particular family member you are targeting. Keep in mind that there is no one-size-fits-all opening. In fact, when your relationship with your parents features multiple problematic patterns that are not merely different manifestations of the same CCRT, you may need to devise a separate strategy for each of them.

The five strategies are:

1. Begin with family history and show how it led to current problems.

2. Confront your parent directly about a current interaction.

3. Express worries about a parent directly.

4. Counter distancing behavior by expressing a desire for a good relationship.

5. Ask for advice about a problem you and your parent share.

Let's look at each of these in detail.

Opening Strategy 1. Begin with Family History and Show How It Led to Current Problems

Some parents are more comfortable talking about the distant past than they are talking about what is going on between the two of you right now. However, particularly with more dysfunctional families, the exact opposite may true. Some parents do not want to touch their relationships with their own parents with the proverbial ten-foot pole. With them, this strategy is not likely to be effective.

You can open with some questions about family history that you have not asked yet and that might be a bit more touchy. Then you can use the answers as a springboard to discussing even more emotionally charged past family interactions that seem somewhat analogous to the current ICDD problem. Current problems can be an unacknowledged *subtext* during these conversations about the past.

Slowly move forward in time to discuss more and more recent events as you trace the history of the family problems into the present. This can, in turn, lead to a discussion about all the ways they have come to affect your current relationship with this parent, and how it has led to the current problems. In doing so, be careful to avoid seeming to attack or blame any of the players in the family drama.

Kaylee's Story: Resentfully Intrusive

Kaylee was fed up with the ICDD behavior of her mother, Joanne: her constant criticisms, repeated concerns about the wisdom of Kaylee's life choices, and daily phone calls to check up and aggressively pry. Joanne's behavior was particularly annoying because she always acted as if Kaylee was a big burden that she was forced to bear.

Kaylee learned the story behind this behavior during an interview with an uncle, one of Joanne's four younger siblings. These siblings now mostly avoided Joanne because they felt she was "too bossy." When Joanne was fifteen, their father had been disabled in a workplace accident and died a short time later. Their mother had been forced to go to work full time in a low-paying job. In turn, Joanne was forced to stop pursuing her own dreams in order to assume the caretaking role for her younger siblings.

Kaylee formed a hypothesis about the conflict behind her mother's behavior: that Joanne continues to feel a strong need to play the role of caretaker that was forced on her—as this was the life script chosen for her by her family—but she covertly resents the role. Furthermore, Joanne probably envies Kaylee her independence and freedom to do whatever she wants. But she criticizes Kaylee's ability to do this well, because by judging those choices as problematic, Joanne can justify her own choice in life to follow the family script.

Kaylee invited her mother to lunch at a quiet local restaurant. Typically, Joanne soon began to criticize Kaylee, in this case for having taken a trip with her boyfriend instead of immediately tending to some other business in her life. "Those things should have taken precedence over gallivanting around," she opined.

Instead of silently stewing about her mother's negativity, as she had in the past, Kaylee agreed that in some circumstances her mother's advice surely would be a wise choice (a countermove, "The Kernel of Truth," described in chapter 6). She then used that as a jumping-off point to bring up Joanne's relevant past. She first expressed empathy for her grandmother's quandary before trying to move the story forward to her mother's own predicament.

"I heard from Uncle Gabriel that your mother was certainly in no position to do anything like taking a spontaneous trip. I can't imagine what things must have been like for her after Grandpa passed away."

Kaylee's mother frowned and suddenly became silent.

Kaylee pressed on: "She had to go to work, right? With all those mouths to feed. That sounds so intense. How did all of you handle it?"

Joanne looked perturbed. "You have to do what you have to do, you know? Actually, what do you know? You've always had it so easy." This was an overt change in subject. Kaylee recognized it, and did not take the bait, but pressed on with discussing the relevant family history.

"Well, you certainly didn't have it easy, that's for sure! It sounds like when Grandma had to go to work, you had no choice but to take care of your younger siblings. Since you were so young yourself, you must have felt pretty powerless to keep it all under control. And with all that responsibility!"

Joanne began to tear up—something Kaylee had never seen before. But she quickly composed herself and then, in a voice almost stripped of emotion, said, "Yeah, that was pretty tough."

Kaylee then moved the discussion forward in time. "And then when I was younger and Grandma got sick, you had to take care of her while at the same time being in charge of a husband and kids. That must have been so much responsibility."

"No shit, Sherlock," Joanne shot back. Again, Kaylee did not take the bait of responding to the not-so-subtle insult.

"Well, I never knew about much of this. I'm sorry I didn't realize how difficult it was for you."

Having acknowledged her mother's struggle, Kaylee then moved to the present and what might be behind their current problematic interactions: "I wonder—is that why you always feel you have to take on the burden of checking up on me all the time? I'm sure you aren't trying to confuse me, but you always seem unhappy about having to do that—but also compelled to do it anyway." As she said this, despite her best efforts, Kaylee sounded angry. They had reached the stage where the current dilemma her mother faced was under discussion, but unfortunately, Kaylee was not quite successful in controlling her tone of voice.

Joanne snapped back: "You never appreciate half of what I've done to keep you from screwing up your life!" Kaylee realized she'd made an error. In response, she again used the strategy of looking for the kernel of truth in Joanne's angry and invalidating statement. She knew she needed to admit the obvious fact that she was indeed angry with her mother, and explain why without getting defensive.

"Well, Mom, I do get annoyed sometimes that you seem to have so little faith in me. It's like you doubt you did a good job in raising me, when I thought you really did an amazing job of making me who I am today."

Joanne's eyes widened. After a moment of silence, she suddenly put down her fork. "It's getting late, and I have to be going."

Kaylee knew she had made progress, and that the conversation could more easily be continued at a later date.

*"Well, Mom, I'm glad we had a chance to talk about this.
Let's pick this up another time."*

*Joanne rolled her eyes, but she kissed Kaylee goodbye. Later
on, they were in fact able to have a conversation about whether
or not Joanne needed to continue her old role now that things
had changed. Kaylee was then in a position to request changes
in their relationship.*

Opening Strategy 2. Confront the Parent Directly About a Current Interaction

With this opening, you cut to the chase and move directly into
a tactful confrontation about how your parent's behavior adversely
affects you. The term "confrontation," as I am using it here, despite
its usual connotation, means *bravely bringing up a problem for
discussion*—not picking a fight. In fact—and this is crucial—if a
direct confrontation is to succeed, there can be no sense whatsoever
that the conversation is an adversarial proceeding. You must remain
resolutely empathic—a tall order, I know—and say nothing that
even remotely suggests your parents are morally to blame for your
problems or that your own behavior has nothing at all to do with an
issue. When it comes to dysfunctional interactions, neither of the
propositions "It's all my fault" nor "I had nothing to do with it" is
ever remotely accurate. It takes two to tango.

To remain empathic, it helps to remind yourself that, despite all
appearances to the contrary, your parents probably already feel guilty
about how they have been treating you. They just cannot acknowledge that without revealing something they feel they must hide
about themselves. Furthermore, their guilt makes them want to push
you away even more, since they probably think you are better off
without them.

Anything that increases their sense of guilt will lead to more
denial, not less. Yet you still need to bring up any problem you have
with how they behave. One strategy that effectively resolves this

catch-22 is to start the confrontation by employing a disclaimer and then acknowledging their dilemma; for example: "Dad, I know you always wanted me to succeed in my career, but when you did not come to my graduation, I began to wonder if for some reason you might feel threatened by my success."

You can also constructively acknowledge your own contribution to any earlier misunderstanding by explaining that your behavior was due to your having *misread* their motives, at least to some degree. You just did not completely understand what was going on! This admission can even lead to more revealing discussions of the past family history that led to shared internal conflicts in the first place.

Geneva's Story: Mean, Then Distant

Geneva's relationship with her mother, Madelyn, was characterized by periods of togetherness alternated with periods of estrangement. Every time their relationship seemed to start improving, the mother would start to do nasty, almost despicable things that would absolutely infuriate Geneva. For example, several times she had spread untruths about Geneva to other relatives. When confronted, Madelyn would simply deny that she had done what she had done.

The last instance seemed to be the final straw. Madelyn had strongly hinted to Geneva's new boyfriend that Geneva was having an affair with one of her male coworkers, and this almost led to the couple's breaking up. Madelyn then denied she had said anything to him. After that, even though Geneva and Madelyn lived in the same city a mere two miles apart, they were estranged for several years with no communication at all between them—until Geneva decided to bite the bullet and try to solve the issue once and for all.

Geneva's only clue about the origins of her mother's distancing behavior was that she had seen Madelyn treat her own father, Geneva's grandfather, in a similar way, although he seemed to have done nothing to deserve such treatment. In fact, he had always seemed to come back for more.

When Geneva called, Madelyn acted in her typical manner after a period of estrangement: she launched into a breezy, newsy conversation as if they had been on speaking terms the whole time—and as if nothing untoward had ever occurred. Geneva soon started the confrontation, using a disclaimer in anticipation of Madelyn's feigning ignorance about why they had not been talking.

She said, "Mom, I know you want a close relationship with me, but every time we start to get close, you again do things that you know are really going to piss me off, and then you lie to me about it. I don't understand why you do that."

"Like, what have I done?"

On hearing this, Geneva felt her usual anger and frustration—even though it was exactly what she had expected. She knew she had to keep those feelings in check to deal effectively with her mother's typical denials. Using a matter-of-fact, nonscolding tone of voice, she said, "We've talked about that a million times. There is no point in getting into examples again or arguing about the obvious. You and I both know exactly what I'm talking about."

"No, really, I don't. Like what?

Geneva refused to be drawn in to an unwinnable argument but did not want to start another extended estrangement. So she said, "Well, I'd really like to discuss this, so when you are ready to do that, please call me back." That was meant to make certain she had done nothing to foreclose on the possibility of continuing the conversation.

But her mother shot back, "Why do you always blame everything on me? Besides, it's all in the past." With this response Madelyn was, without hesitation and without acknowledging anything she had done, starting a whole new argument. In fact, she was throwing up two defenses simultaneously. This was meant to splinter the conversation's primary focus: Madelyn's distancing behavior.

Geneva brought the subject right back, using Madelyn's "all in the past" comment while just ignoring the blame issue: "I disagree. You never stop doing it. I want to make sure it never happens again. You act really warm and nice for a while, and then when I am least expecting it, you start up again."

Madelyn again feigned ignorance. (Parents can be stubborn this way.) "Start up with what?" she asked innocently.

"There you go again."

At this point, since the strategies Madelyn had been using were not working, she suddenly employed yet a different one: Mea Culpa. She started to sob inconsolably: "I know. I've been just an awful mom to you."

Geneva had seen her mother do this before, and she was prepared. She used the strategy of expressing puzzlement: "Well, your reaction right now tells me you really do feel bad about doing this to me, but then you keep doing it again and again. I'm mystified as to why you keep doing that. And I have noticed that you seem to do the same thing with Grandpa."

"Grandpa? Well, he thrives on that!"

"Huh?" Geneva was taken aback—and felt a strong urge to tell her mother how crazy that sounded. She wanted to defend her grandpa, but then she realized she had just been presented with a clue that might nail the family dynamics that motivated her mother's distancing. "Really?" she asked, genuinely curious. "I'd like to hear more about what you mean."

Geneva never was able to uncover the reason why her mother had taken on the role of the "evil bitch" in her own family of origin, but as we will discuss in the next chapter, she was eventually able to establish a continued relationship with Madelyn—something her mother indeed really wanted— contingent on certain conditions.

Opening Strategy 3. Express Worries About a Parent Directly

If you have been sacrificing your own idiosyncratic ambitions or other relationships in order to overtly look after one or both of your parents, this strategy may work for you. In family therapy circles, this is called being a "parentified child." You may be on call to do shopping for a parent who refuses to learn how to drive, to help mediate your parents' disputes with one another, or to provide missing companionship for one of them. They may have health problems and insist you take care of them and do things like take them to doctor appointments.

In a sense, all of the ways in which children attempt to stabilize their parents' functioning involve the adult child's taking care of a parent—even avoiding subjects that might trigger the parent's insecurities about their own behavior. The situation I am discussing here, however, is one in which the caretaker role is not covert but out in the open. It is usually obvious to anyone who knows what is really going on, although the family may have mechanisms for keeping the true nature of the situation away from the prying eyes of outsiders.

For instance, in families with a member conflicted over the issue of being dependent versus being independent, an unemployed adult son may live with, or near, a widowed mother. The mother acts in private as if she is completely dependent on him, although to outsiders the adult child appears to be the dependent one—mostly on his mother for her money. I refer to this odd shell game of managing perceptions as a game of "Who's taking care of whom?"

In most cases, neither of you directly acknowledges your caretaking role in conversation, so initiating this strategy requires that you make it the *overt subject* of a conversation. This is how you start working on the task of letting a parent fend more for herself, allowing you to extricate yourself from your caretaking role and start to live your own life. Most parents really are perfectly capable of self-care and covertly would actually be happier if the caretaker would bow out. Even if a parent needs some help due to physical infirmities, this does not usually have to be a full-time job. If your parents are having marital problems and you are running interference for them in some way, your behavior is truly getting in the way of their ability to address their own issues head on—which makes things worse for them in the long run. Not to mention taking up way too much of your time.

Typically the best way to execute this strategy is to start by saying you are worried about your parent's well-being in some way. You might say something like, "I've been really worried about you lately, Mom. You've looked so lonely and depressed," or "Dad, I'm really concerned that you and Mom are at each other's throats." You must make this statement *without any suggestions or any advice* to your parent about how to take care of this problem. This is critical for three reasons. First, your giving advice makes it very easy for a parent to sidetrack the issue by arguing with (or "yes-butting") any particular counsel you offer. He can dissect and debate your behavioral prescriptions ad infinitum. Second, chances are good that any advice you may give is something fairly obvious. If you "go parental" with such advice, you are also insulting your parent's intelligence. Third, you are putting yourself right back in the parental child role from which you are trying to extricate yourself.

Your opening expression of concern with this strategy conveys the message "I've been trying to help you [feel better, or solve your problems]." You will eventually address the fact that your efforts are not really working.

A parent's initial response will probably be, "You don't have to worry about me; I'm doing fine." He is expressing covert parental guilt over the position he has put you in. Once again, he really does feel bad about it but cannot totally dismiss you from your role without revealing his underlying conflict. At the same time, it is an expression of his underlying resentment that his family role requires him to think of himself as inadequate in some way when he really wants to be independent. Unfortunately, this statement also invalidates you, because it dismisses your legitimate worries while denying that his dependent behavior is, in fact, a problem for you. It also invalidates your caring and concern.

Your best response here is: "I appreciate the fact that you don't want me to trouble myself with or worry about your problems, but I really am concerned."

The parent may then counter with a distancing remark such as, "No, you don't. You don't care about anyone but yourself!"

You can answer this type of statement by coming back with a sincere sounding, "I wish there were some way to convince you that I really do care." Then refuse to argue that point further—because there's simply no way you can prove how much you care one way or another about anything.

When you're stuck in the "who is taking care of whom" game just described, another possible opening for strategy #3 is a statement such as, "Mom, I know that you are perfectly capable of taking care of yourself, but sometimes you seem to be afraid to do that for some reason." With this opening gambit, your mother has an obvious comeback she can use to avoid facing the dilemma that you have brought up—usually for the first time. She can point out that *you* are really the dependent one.

And she may have a legitimate point. After all, you may have, to date, seemed to be psychologically incapable of going out and making your own life separate from Mom's money. Some people in this situation have allowed the parent to bail them out of one financial bind after another, for the covert purpose of allowing a mom to indulge her secret, forbidden desire to be a person in charge of someone. This being the case, the child reasons, *Who am I to be talking about Mom's dependency problem?* If you are in this situation, the counterstrategy is to admit to the kernel of truth. You *have* done those things. Explain why you have acted the way you have: you have not striven for independence as much as you should have thus far because of your continued worries about how your mother might feel if she were left alone and on her own.

If you are successful at getting your parent to talk frankly about your expressed areas of concern, the two of you can then go on to discuss how you both have been misreading one another's intentions, discuss the past family history that led to the problem, and begin to reset your respective roles to what they should be.

Leon's Story: A Cycle of Need

Let us return to the case of Leon and Gracie from chapter 2. Gracie was constantly nagging her son, without any regard for his personal life, to take care of household chores that she could really do herself. Then she would criticize his work.

Leon tried opening metacommunication with a disclaimer, and then framing his concern as puzzlement. "Gee, Mom, I know you are not trying to confuse me, but you always seem to need me to come over and do things for you, and then you seem completely unhappy about it. I'm really concerned that something is really bothering you and making you unhappy, but I am not sure exactly what. I wonder if you're not sure, yourself, if you really like being dependent on men, but you think you're supposed to be."

The mother had a backup response to get Leon to stop talking about this problem. She ignored his hypothesis about a potential internal conflict leading to these double messages, and tried to change the subject. "Oh, Leon, you're so sweet," she cooed, suddenly becoming all warm. "But isn't that what families are for—to help each other out? Don't you remember, when you needed money last year, you came to me?"

Leon had heard her make similar statements a long time before, and it had really stuck in his head. So he was ready. He used her statement to bridge right back to his hypothesis. "Well, Mom, I'm glad you brought that up. That's another reason why I worry about you, and also why I am confused about what I'm supposed to do. You always, at least at first, beam when you get to be the one who's in charge, so I let you bail me out. However, at the same time, it almost seems like you are afraid of being the one in charge."

Gracie's warm tone suddenly turned sarcastic. She shot back, "Oooh, aren't you being the amateur shrink!"

Leon realized that despite the sarcasm, she really did not address whether being an amateur shrink was a good or a bad thing.

"I know," he admitted with a knowing smile, "because I've been thinking a lot about what you've said about the way you were brought up, which led to the question I just asked you. It sounds like this is hard for you to talk about, but I really think we need to clear the air about this so we can figure out what to do about it."

Opening Strategy 4. Counter Distancing Behavior by Expressing a Desire for a Good Relationship

This strategy is useful for parents who have used mild to moderate distancing behavior primarily to put a stop to any of your attempts to get close to them, or to discuss important family issues. In these cases, the parents usually have met the child's previous attempts at problem solving with hostility, escalation of their provocative behavior, or even verbal abuse.

To begin with this strategy, first express your wish for more closeness with your parent. You can say something like, "I really feel bad that we don't seem to get along very well; I really wish that things were better between us." This statement tends to soften up a parent right off the bat, and therefore can elicit an initial positive reaction. Here's why.

For one, the statement appeals to the side of the parent's ambivalence that you wish were the dominant one: the side that really does desire a close relationship with you. Your expressed desire for closeness with your parents in spite of the fact that they have been treating you badly communicates your great love for them.

The other reason is a lot more subtle. Many distancing parents do not like to admit that their behavior is intended on purpose to drive you away. Their blatant rejection of this overture would be, in effect, an implicit admission that this is exactly what they are doing.

If your parents respond positively to your desire for a better relationship, you can wonder aloud why you and they seem to be fighting so often. This question can again lead to empathic discussions of the nature and origins of mixed messages and misunderstandings in the relationship, which you can in turn use as a basis for requesting concrete behavioral changes.

Alexandra's Story: Disappearing Acts

Alexandra was challenged to balance her blossoming career with taking care of her sick children, who had a partially disabling genetic condition that ran in her mother's family. When it came to helping Alexandra with these competing responsibilities, her parents routinely gave her mixed messages that were both highly invalidating and aggravating. For example, once they insisted on taking care of her kids when she was set to go on a big job interview, but at the last minute they suddenly took off and left town. Alexandra ended up having to cancel the interview right before it was supposed to take place and lost out on what might have been a great opportunity.

Her parents defended their sudden decision to travel with a lame excuse: "The hotel we've been wanting to stay at offered such a great deal, we couldn't pass it up." As usual, Alexandra lost her temper and screamed at them for being thoughtless and uncaring louses who did not really give a crap about their own daughter or, for that matter, their grandchildren. Because of this type of interaction, the tension at family events was frequently palpable.

Alexandra decided to first employ strategy #4 with her father, Grayson. She started with the standard opening: "Dad, I really feel bad that we don't seem to get along very well; I really

wish that things were better between us." She had practiced with
a tape recorder to make certain she sounded as sincere in that
sentiment as humanly possible.

Alexandra thought she perceived a momentary look of
discomfort pass across Grayson's face. "Oh really?" he finally
said. "It seems to me like you want to see us as little as possible
and think we're really horrible."

"Well, of course I've been avoiding you," Alexandra
admitted. "That's because things always seem to be so tense
when we get together. Do you have any idea why that keeps
happening?"

Grayson had no answer, so Alexandra went ahead and
offered a hypothesis. "I had a thought about what is going on
with us, and I was wondering what you'd think about it. I seem
to recall that when I was a kid, your mother, who was usually a
fiercely independent businesswoman, would always seem to 'get
sick' just as we were about to leave on vacation, and suddenly
demand your help. You would then have to cancel our trip. I
wonder if we are, like, trapped inside of some sort of
Groundhog Day family life...or something."

Grayson's demeanor softened considerably, and he seemed
intrigued. As if he'd been thinking about this for a long time, he
started talking about his own frustration with his hypochondriac
mother. He then added, "Maybe you're on to something."

Unfortunately, in some families, your expressing a wish for closeness may lead to an unexpected, extremely nasty, and particularly
devastating rejection of you that is worse than anything that may
have come before. Your parent may respond with a statement that
communicates the sentiment, "Well, I do not want to be close to
you; in fact, I wish you had never been born." This response immediately tells you not only that this strategy will not work, but also
that the family dysfunction is probably far more severe than you
thought. You will in most instances require the assistance of a therapist. Nonetheless, if you do hear this from your parents, keep in

mind it is unlikely that they really feel that way. They say this because they are feeling desperate to push you away so they can avoid something in themselves, and they probably think you are better off being away from them. If you had not been born, neither they nor you would be in this predicament.

Opening Strategy 5. Ask for Advice About a Problem You and Your Parent Share

If you are following in your parent's footsteps in some way, this strategy could work. You may have recreated your parent's maladaptive behavior in your own career or relationships in order to shield your parent from feelings of envy. You may have appeared to try, but failed to achieve, some goal that is desperately desired by but forbidden to your parent. This often happens after a parent has spent years ambivalently trying to shield you from this very outcome, encouraging you to be everything he was not, or from making the same mistakes he did. His actions, which speak louder than his words, seem to say otherwise.

A good initial move is for you to ask your parent for advice about how to handle a difficulty that you are experiencing *outside* of your relationship with that parent, but which closely parallels a difficulty the parent has also experienced. For example, in a family in which the father has always given in to the mother's demands, regardless of how reasonable they were, a daughter may come to the mother with the following request for help: "Mom, I need your advice. My husband is following me around like a puppy dog and never wants to make any important decisions. How do you think I should handle it?"

The goal here is to for you to establish a sense of common ground with your parent from which to work toward change. Usually, when parallels between your behavior and your parent's come up in conversation, one party ends up criticizing the other for that person's behavior—even though you both are doing almost the same things.

The criticized party feels that the other party is being a huge hypocrite and reacts negatively, and mutual anger and defensiveness begin to spiral out of control.

This strategy prevents that because it changes the valence of your interactions over shared issues from negative to positive in two ways. First, since you are *admitting* to having the same problem or something similar yourself, your parent will not feel as criticized. After all, how can you be critical of your parent if you have the same problem? Second, it puts you and your parent in the proper hierarchy, avoiding any potential role reversals. You are asking, say, your mother for advice based on her experience and intelligence.

The common problem may then be used as a springboard to an open discussion about how any parallels in the family's relationship patterns came about, which allows you to bring up a hypothesis based on your research into the family background. Discussions of the nature and origins of mixed messages and misunderstandings in your relationship may suggest ways to stop them from continuing.

Natalia's Story: Inevitable Breadwinners

The family dynamics of Natalia and her mother, Stella, were somewhat similar to those of Kara and Nicole in chapter 6. Both mother and daughter had a strong tendency to pick irresponsible male partners and support them financially. When Natalia was a teenager, her parents divorced due to Stella's frustration with her husband, but then she kept bringing home unemployed or underemployed boyfriends. If Natalia questioned her mother about her choice in men, the mother would justify each new one by protesting that she was with him simply because she loved him despite his flaws, and felt that it was therefore her duty to bring home the bacon, so to speak, if he would not.

Nonetheless, she would frequently complain about the guy's laziness. If Natalia dared echo those complaints, however, Stella would shift gears and start to defend him. Notably, Stella was clearly frustrated with the men she chose, which led to her relationships being relatively short term.

Natalia fell for a man named Gregory and later married him. As she thought about her own reactions, Natalia began to wonder if she were somehow following in her mother's footsteps. Gregory worked at a low-paying job that was far beneath his capabilities. He seemed to prefer spending time with his slacker friends to being with her, and he also spent money profligately, like an immature teenager whose parents could never say no to him.

She also began to pay closer attention to her mother's attitude about Gregory's behavior, and noted some odd contradictions. Natalia was not completely sure, but her mother seemed to her to be, if anything, amused by Gregory's behavior. She would laugh about it and make snide comments. However, whenever Natalia seemed unhappy during those times when Greg was not there for her, Stella would invalidate Natalia's feelings by defending or excusing him. "Well, he's okay. Be glad he's not like your father, anyway. It's not really a big deal."

Taking a shot at Natalia's dad was not unusual for Stella, and this presented some specific challenges. Natalia still had warm feelings for her father despite his being somewhat of a deadbeat dad, and she had a tendency to defend him. She knew that if Stella were to say something critical of him during metacommunication about Stella's attitude toward Greg, she would have to bite her tongue. Otherwise, her mother could easily accuse her of being a hypocrite: how could Natalia defend her father and then criticize her mother for defending Greg? Although Stella's relationship with Natalia's father was different in many respects from Natalia's relationship with Greg, there were some fairly obvious and consequential similarities.

Natalia had also realized that, in the past, she had experienced deep anxiety whenever she dated responsible guys, for fear that her mother would see that and get depressed. She was not sure exactly what she had seen in her mother to make her feel that way, but the feeling had been very strong.

Natalia and her mother had frequent coffee dates, and she decided to employ this strategy at the next one. Stella was between boyfriends, which seemed to be a plus—they would avoid the complication of introducing yet another man's behavior into the conversation. There's never a perfect time for metacommunication, but this timing was pretty close.

"Mom, I need your advice. I know Gregory has a lot of positive qualities, but he's neglecting me a lot, as well as sending us into the poorhouse with his reckless spending habits. I don't really want a divorce, but this is starting to be intolerable. What do you think I should do?"

Stella's initial defense was to invoke fatalism. "Well, you might as well just put up with it. I think you'll find that better men are few and far between, and there's nothing you can do to change any of them."

Natalia employed the recommended countermove. "Ya know, I have thought that's true a lot of the time myself. But I am beginning to question whether it really is. Some of the married women at work seem to have avoided that problem. Their husbands are good men, and when they are upset with them, they bring it up, and seem to be able to negotiate some solution. Do you think the fact that we both have ended up with sorta weak men, and we never make any demands on them, is just bad luck—or something else?"

"Well, there are a few good men you can do that with out there somewhere. But I think finding that needle in a haystack is generally a lost cause."

"Gee, Mom, I'm surprised to hear you say that. You often do not put up with that kind of treatment. You must have thought there was something better."

"Hope springs eternal, I guess."

"I was wondering if anyone else in your family seemed to think that all men are losers and that you just have to put up with it?"

"Why do you ask?"

"*Well, maybe we're following some kind of strange rule that our family sticks to for some reason.*"

With that, Stella's interest was piqued. Natalia was able to share some of what she had put together from what she had heard about the family's history, and later she told Stella her concerns about how Stella might react if she was able to solve the problem with Gregory.

EXERCISE: Choose a Strategy and Plan for What Might Go Wrong

Now you have seen several possible approaches to ICDD problem resolution and you are familiar with ways to counter the usual tricks your parents might use to derail such conversations. You also know some things about the origins of these problems. So you are in an excellent position to alter the course of your relationships with your parents. Start this exercise by reviewing the initiating strategies described in this chapter and thinking about how your parents might respond to each of them.

First, consider whether you have tried a version of any of these strategies before without success. Where did the conversation go wrong, and why might your parents have become offended or defensive? When making the latter determination, consider whether you may have triggered their negative reaction by inducing them to feel frightened, attacked, invalidated, or misunderstood.

For any strategies that seem completely new to you, ask yourself which of the various defenses described in chapter 6 they might throw at you in response. Let your mind wander, and write down anything that occurs to you, regardless of whether it seems relevant now.

As you ponder which strategy to choose, keep in mind that, since you have lived with and observed your parents much of your life, you are undoubtedly better at predicting their responses than you might think. Anticipate what might go wrong, and prepare for it. Ask yourself, *How might they react poorly to anything I am considering saying?* and *What have they done or said to me on several occasions that might come into play?*

If you have absolutely no idea how they might respond to any particular strategy, this might mean that they would not know how to respond themselves, and might just appear dumbfounded. This is a clue that the strategy is one you should strongly consider, because it may force your parents to stop reacting in ways they have relied on and start seriously thinking about what you have been saying.

If you have enlisted your spouse, ask them to role-play your parents as discussed in chapter 7. Have them try to respond to the various options in any negative ways that they may have seen coming from your parents.

If the ways you think your parents might respond seem problematic, do not give up on that strategy just yet. First, consider a better way to phrase your initial intervention or another good move to counter the last move. If nothing seems to work, then consider a different initiating strategy and repeat the exercise.

Once you have come up with a plan, practice, practice, and practice some more before approaching your parent.

All five of these opening strategies, as well as any other creative approaches you can devise, are meant to soften up your parents, so to speak, so that all of you can discuss and clarify the family dynamics. Once you and your parents have a better understanding of what is creating and maintaining a problematic relationship pattern, you are ready to address the changes you want to see in your relationship. This is the subject of the next chapter.

CHAPTER 9

Request Specific Changes

After you have completed reading this book and then initiated metacommunication, applied your preplanned countermoves, and thoroughly discussed your misunderstandings and shared conflicts to sort them out, you will then be in a position to pivot the discussion toward changes. How would you like the relationship to proceed?

Of course, when you ask for any behaviors to stop, your parents may again ask you to come up with examples of their behaviors that are problematic for you. Here you risk triggering yet another round of nitpicking discussions or debates about what those behaviors are, precisely; whether you are misinterpreting things; or even whether any of them occur often enough to be a big issue. Your first move to cut this off is to just remind them of your earlier conversations. If that does not work, be patient. Make use of any of the same countermove strategies that you used successfully earlier on to counter any nitpicking.

Natalia's Story: Arriving at Mutual Solutions

After Natalia let her mother, Stella, know that she feared that her mother might get depressed if Natalia were to somehow be able to motivate Gregory to grow up, Stella became defensive. "Do you really think I wouldn't be happy for you? That I'd be jealous of you? I can't believe you would think that of me!"

Natalia: "Ooh, I see what you mean. That was terrible phrasing on my part. I'm so sorry. I know you always want the best for me, and that you are not a jealous person. Now that you point that out, I guess I'd just be concerned that I might become a passive reminder of the problems you've had."

Stella: "I'm sure I could handle that."

Natalia: "You're right. But I should let you know that when I complain about Gregory and you start defending him and brushing off my concerns, I start to think—wrongly or rightly—that you want me to just put up with his irresponsibility. So I am asking you to please consider not doing that. You of all people know what it's like to be in that situation. Maybe instead we could put our heads together and come up with a better plan for negotiating with our men."

Changing the ICDD Reflex

The most important change you will request is simple: that when a CCRT becomes an issue, they refrain from engaging in ICDD behaviors. Instead of just acting out, you can tell your parents that you would like to solve any problems that come up stemming from a CCRT issue by referring back to your previous conversations about family dynamics and then engaging in problem solving. Here are some questions you can pose to your parents:

- How can we alter our reactions so that we do not invalidate one another?

- How can we both become more aware of each other's sensitivities?

- How can we constructively negotiate major differences in outlook?

The solutions involve recognizing the urge to resort to old behaviors, becoming curious about what old conflicts might be arising, and then discussing fears, conflicts, and hopes—without impinging on any of your rights to live your own lives the way each of you sees fit.

Of course, *you* will have to do this as well. This is an excellent time to let your parents know how you hope you will respond when they feel you are doing something invalidating or insensitive to *them.* Tell them you will try your best not to immediately react negatively and will instead think carefully about whether or not they might actually have a good case. You will look for the validity of their feelings and concerns, and you'll try to adjust what you are doing accordingly.

In tense situations, you do not have to agree with their assessment of you—nor do they always have to agree with your assessment of them. Mere disagreement is not the same as invalidation. Two people can hold opposing viewpoints without either one telling the other person that her views have absolutely no merit, are stupid or crazy, or are based on self-delusion. You can deal constructively with one another's perceptions.

Kaylee's Story: Understanding Leads to Change

Soon after Kaylee's initial attempts at metacommunication with her mother, Joanne, at the first opportune moment when they were alone together, Kaylee brought up their prior conversation:

Kaylee: "Mom, I was wondering if you had any more thoughts about our conversation when we last went out to lunch together."

Joanne: "Well, actually I did. I know I'm a worrywart, and believe it or not, I end up getting mad at myself about that. Maybe I do drive you a little crazy. You should have said something to me about it sooner."

Kaylee: "I should have, but I always chickened out. Frankly, I'm a bit of a worrywart myself, you know, and I was worried I would upset you. Hearing that story about your past from Uncle Gabriel made me appreciate how much you are just concerned about me."

Joanne: *(with a smile)* "Gabriel always did have a big mouth."

Kaylee: *(ignoring that last comment)* "I wonder if you feel that every time I mess up, it's because of some sort of failure on your part."

Joanne: *(tearing up a little, nodding)*

Kaylee: "How do you think we should handle this in the future? I will be making my own choices, but when you start to worry about me, could you maybe just tell me about any concerns you might have, rather than checking up on me all the time and imagining the worst? I'll do my best to take your concerns into account, although I can't promise that we'll always agree about them."

Joanne: "I suppose I could try to do that. But it's just so second nature to me to jump on you when I'm worried."

Kaylee: "Old habits are hard to break. Can I just let you know when I think you might be overdoing it? I promise to try not to sound all judgmental about it."

Joanne: *(nodding agreement, appearing to seriously consider this change)*

Kaylee: "Great! I'm getting my nails done tomorrow. Wanna join me? My treat."

Set Boundaries to Prevent ICDD Interactions

You will need to fill any void left by the absence of ICDD behavior. Discuss other aspects of your relationship, such as what your limits are. This will help you avoid ICDD interactions. Explain how you are going to respond if they refuse to stop old patterns: you are going to point these out. Remind them of your past metacommunication conversations and of what they have previously agreed to do and not do.

If you become concerned that you will start to respond with some of your old angry, invalid, critical, and dysfunctional reactions, do what therapists call *setting boundaries*. The emphasis during ongoing boundary setting at this point is not on telling your parents what to do, but on you reacting in a new way to any new instances of their past troublesome behavior. Through the metacommunication you have already accomplished, you can draw on previous empathic discussions of the family CCRTs, which makes setting boundaries much easier.

To establish boundaries in the heat of the moment, you can apply the fallback strategies from chapter 4 for when you lose empathy, and leave the door open for further discussions later. These strategies include letting your parents know that if you feel like you are going to lose it, you will tell them you're going to leave or hang up, and then expressing hope that everyone will handle things better when you've all calmed down. You can do this as often as necessary, in as many separate conversations as you need.

Successful metacommunication can be difficult in the moment, but it will often lead to a satisfying result in which you and your parents achieve a reconciliation, and they begin to behave in ways that show respect for your adulthood, your independence, and your right to make your own choices without being punished or buffeted about by ICDD interactions.

Geneva's Story: Agreeing on Boundaries

As described earlier, Geneva was never able to get her mother, Madelyn, to open up about the history behind the way Madelyn treated both her and her grandfather, so that Geneva could understand the purpose it served. This made trying to empathize with her when she acted in those ways difficult if not impossible. Furthermore, Geneva also knew she could not count on her mother to keep her word about not engaging in distancing and alienating in the future, as Madelyn's seemingly improved behavior could change back at any moment.

Geneva decided that, in order to have a relationship with her mother, she would have to merely let Madelyn know that she would limit contact, and that she was never going to be able to trust her completely.

Over the phone, she said to her mother, "Look, I know you care about me, but something stops you from letting us stay close. In the future, I am probably never again going to be able to trust you not to stab me in the back. I still want to have a relationship—even though I suspect that you might think that I am better off without you in my life—and I also think you really want us to keep in contact."

Madelyn: "Wait, what do you mean, 'stabbing you in the back'?"

Geneva: "Remember what I said before, Mom? I am not going to argue about examples when both you and I know exactly what I'm talking about. I wouldn't want to insult your intelligence in that way."

Madelyn: "All right, all right! Have it your way! So can we at least call each other once in a while?"

Geneva: "You just read my mind, Mom. I'd like to talk to you about what's going on in our lives every couple of weeks or so. But I will not come to visit you at your house, and I won't allow you to come to mine. I'm not going to be a contact with you on social media, and if I find out that you have send friend requests to my friends, I will limit our contact further. Maybe we can go out to eat together once in a while. But I'm afraid I'm always going to be acting somewhat suspicious of you, even when you are being nice. You can talk to me about this if and when that bothers you, and I will listen, but I can't make any promises."

Negotiating the Future

No one type of relationship is right for everyone, so I cannot make any specific recommendations for you or anyone else regarding what your new relationship with your parents will or should look like once the ICDD elements have been taken out of the equation. Nor can I predict the eventual evolution of your relationship with your parents.

You may all decide that you want a somewhat distant but cordial relationship, or you may try to get closer and enjoy one another's company in a variety of specific situations, or you all may aim for a little of each. You can ask for anything from your relationship with them that you genuinely want. You do not have to compare yourself to anyone else, or second-guess your own desires. The only necessity is that the relationship with your parents be honest, and that there be at least some relatively pleasant interactions from time to time or when necessary.

Honest disagreements between you and your parents that are *not* the result of ambivalence over rules enforcing family homeostasis are inevitable. No two people agree on everything—not even close. You and they will no doubt not always see eye to eye over what you value in life, or over politics or social issues. In these situations, agreeing to disagree and just avoiding those issues for the most part in your interactions is a perfectly fine outcome.

Alexandra's Story: Acknowledging a Parent's Limits

When we last followed Alexandra's story, she had gotten her dad, Grayson, to talk about his frustration with his own mother, and she offered a hypothesis with a disclaimer, some empathy, and an acknowledgment of her own role in the problem: "I know you don't mean to, but at times it feels like you are taking out your anger at your mother on me. I know my needs look overwhelming, what with my having sick children and a demanding career to deal with."

Grayson said, "I don't know how you handle all that!"

Alexandra then suggested what they might do when she was feeling overwhelmed and he was feeling put upon: "You know, you don't always have to volunteer to help me when I need something. I admit that I prefer that you and Mom take care of my kids, because you are familiar with how to handle their illnesses, but I do have other options. Do you think you can tell me when you find my problems a bit too much and you need me to use those options? Now that I am aware of what's going on with you, I'll try to back off."

Exploring Together

So what's the next step in your evolving relationship with your parents? One valuable possible option to consider is working together to expand your knowledge of both your family's genogram material and the CCRTs you have already uncovered. The process is very similar to the one with a spouse or romantic partner described in chapter 4. Having a "relationship about your relationship" with your parents can be a fun and highly enlightening activity.

The family can get together to do more research to further investigate their backgrounds as well as the shared history of their ethnic or cultural group. The goal is to fill in the blanks in the collective genogram. In doing so, the parties may discover previously unknown reasons for their own behavior and reactions. Most of us puzzle at one time or another over some of our recurring reactions in various situations, or over some of the seemingly odd or inappropriate values that our parents imparted to us. Knowing the reasons behind these mysterious feelings, attitudes, and behaviors can make it easier for us to change our own bad habits when doing so had previously been quite difficult.

Leon's Story: Owning the History Affects the Present

When we last left Leon, his mother, Gracie, had accused him of playing amateur shrink when he tried to discuss the double messages he was getting from her. He continued to play "amateur shrink" as if it were the most natural, positive thing in the world one could do. "Look, Mom, I'm not trying to give you a hard time, and I agree family members should help one another out to some degree, but I really am concerned about your feeling bad when you want to be independent. You're such a bright and capable person. I know you don't mean to, but it puts me in a no-win situation. Do you have any idea where that came from?"

Without admitting that Leon was on the right track, Gracie started to talk about her childhood and revealed some facts about her upbringing of which Leon had been unaware. Leon listened intently and then shifted into problem-solving mode:

"Do you think you might be able to think about your feelings a bit more when you start thinking you need to call me to do something and maybe feeling resentful about it underneath? I can tell you that I will bring it up if I feel you are giving me a mixed message about coming over. And if you really do need me

to fix something, I'm letting you know that from now on I'm going to wait until it is a convenient time for me before I come. Otherwise, we are just going to be driving each other crazy. I want us to have a better relationship."

Gracie got quiet and never completely agreed with what Leon had said, but her problematic behavior started to change significantly after that conversation. She very rarely called him over to help her with household tasks.

Now's the Time to Begin Metacommunicating With Your Parent

With this book as your guide, you now have everything you need to metacommunicate. But let me be honest: I can almost guarantee that you will be sorely tempted to keep putting off doing this. Even in the most functional of families, discussing family processes in ways that have never been done before is a daunting prospect. But I can reassure you that most of the time, if you have done your homework, it turns out to be a bit easier than you might have imagined. However, it can turn out to be even more difficult than you thought. Nonetheless, now that you've prepared yourself, it's time to get started while it's fresh in your mind. Do not procrastinate or try to wait until the mythical perfect time. There will always be good excuses available, so push those aside and dive in as soon as you can.

Here are the steps:

1. Pick the parent you think might be the easiest to deal with.

2. Choose the major problematic ICDD interaction you have with this person over a prominent CCRT, and focus on that in your conversation.

3. Set a time and place.

4. Initiate the conversation, using the strategy you have chosen.

5. Employ your prepared countermoves to keep the logic straight and overcome the person's defensive reflexes.

6. Request, firmly but without sounding overly pushy or dictatorial, the changes you would like to see happen.

7. Afterward, write the entire conversation down.

If there is another major repetitive dysfunctional interaction you'll need to address, start the metacommunication process again. Repeat it with each important issue and each important attachment figure.

EXERCISE: Analyze the Conversation to Move Forward

When you write down the entire conversation as best as you can remember it, regardless of whether or not the effort was successful, be sure to include

- how it started and how it ended

- whether your parent reacted positively or negatively

- whether your parent at any point reacted in a way that you did not know how to respond to

Study the conversation closely, looking for signs of your parent's defensiveness, and come up with your best guess about why that may have occurred. Look for any lapses of empathy on your part. See if you and your parent fell right back into an old unproductive pattern. What might you have done differently to prevent that?

Now think about where to go next. Based on how successful your first conversation was, ask yourself:

- What can I do to make the relationship more like I wish it would be?

- How might I steer my parent there?

- Are there other aspects of the problem that have yet to be addressed?

- How might I address them?

You have now seen several ways to engage in problem-solving metacommunication about recurring ICDD interactions so that you can request changes. I hope this chapter has given you some ideas about the possible course the process might take, as well as how you might employ the countermeasures we have discussed.

In the next chapter, we will consider some issues that, although little-known, are important to know about because they may cause a successful effort to unravel. We will discuss what to do in the likely event of family relapses into old habitual patterns. Finally, we'll explore how to take advantage of your newfound opportunity to become self-actualized when you are no longer stuck in a family role.

CHAPTER 10

Overcome Habit and Relapse

When it comes to our social behavior, we are creatures of habit. This is particularly true of our behavior within our families, in which we all have a marked tendency to put the needs of our kin group above our own. Because of this, even after completing successful meta-communication with each of your parents about each major problematic and repetitive ICDD interaction, you need to keep an eye out for certain patterns that may lead everyone, including you, to fall right back into the old dysfunctional ways.

This chapter will discuss patterns that often lead to relapses, and what you can do to get you and your parents back on the preferred track. Whatever happens, you can press forward with a new pattern of self-discovery. We will begin with a particularly frustrating pattern called "the game without end" (Watzlawick et al. 1967). In this game, the person who was asked to change a certain behavior does so—but in an annoying or obnoxious way. Then the person who asked for the change criticizes the changer for doing exactly what he was asked to do. (I do not know why people engaged in the game without end can deny that they have deliberately made the requested change in a way guaranteed to create further problems, but they almost invariably do.) Let's look at how the game transpires.

The Game Without End

In the types of family dysfunction described in this book, you and your parents have probably been locked into several negative, repetitive, and predictable interactions that have taken place over many years. In this ongoing dance, the ways in which you respond to one another have become habitual. The patterns have become compulsive precisely because of their frequency.

This happens similarly to the mutual role function support described in chapter 2, where everyone involved tends to think it is the other people, not them, who want the relationships to continue in their current form. They can see compulsivity in everyone else. But each person involved in the dance overlooks the fact that his or her own behavior practically begs for the same responses from everyone else. So the whole family invariably perpetuates the dysfunction through the responses they each exhibit.

So guess what happens when you tell them you want them to behave differently? Even if they think the new way of relating will be better for them and is therefore desirable, they may still be a little skeptical about *your* motives and intentions. Your previous compulsiveness with the old patterns makes the others doubtful about what you truly want. You *say* you want things to be different, but do you really? Perhaps, as in the case of Geneva's mother, you are trying to lull the others into a false sense of complacency; then, when they least expect it, you will suddenly try to get them to return to the old familiar relationship rules.

Any request you make to change the rules of the game may be seen as perhaps having an ulterior motive. In response, your relative may devise a sort of test to see if you really mean what you say and really want the changes you requested.

Kaylee's Story: Arranging Validation for Nagging

Let's illustrate this with an example from Kaylee's situation with her mother, Joanne. Kaylee wanted her mother to be less intrusive and to quit checking up on her so much, because that behavior seemed to Kaylee to be a vote of no confidence in her ability to take care of herself. After the conversation about the issue, Joanne did, in fact, back off considerably. Without further ado, she backed way off.

In fact, she seemed to stop calling Kaylee much at all. Kaylee still wanted to have a relationship, so her mother's having gone to the opposite extreme was almost as annoying as her old intrusiveness. If Kaylee were to criticize her mother for not calling often enough, Joanne would come to the conclusion that Kaylee—who had always put up with the intrusiveness before—really wanted and needed it. Joanne would then decide that she should go back to her old ways.

Joanne might think to herself, See? She said she wanted me to change, but she really does not want me to at all! *She might explain this to herself by hypothesizing that Kaylee really did need her help but just did not like to admit it. So Joanne did not even show up at Kaylee's house for a party celebrating an important milestone in Kaylee's life. The way Joanne's tricky "test" played out is a classic example of the game without end.*

Countermove: *Praise the Change, Alter the Course*

Fortunately, there's a very effective way to counter the game without end. The trick is to first enthusiastically praise the person for doing what you asked—*before* going on to address the *manner* in which they followed your request. Kaylee employed this strategy by saying to Joanne, in the most pleasant tone she could muster, "Mom, I really appreciate the way you have stopped calling me all the time, worrying about how I'm doing. But that does not mean I don't want to hear from you at all. I hope you didn't get that idea. You are still very important to me."

Full Relapses

Since our brains wire themselves to react automatically and *without thought* to familiar-appearing situations, our old automatic responses can easily be triggered—despite everyone's best efforts to prevent this. Sooner or later, no matter how hard everyone tries, anyone and everyone involved is bound to react automatically and fall back into the old pattern. Changing old habits takes time, patience, and repetition.

Your own old automatic responses may kick in, and you might react with an angry attack or defensiveness. You might be thinking to yourself, *Oh no, here we go again!* and, because of your frustration, you'll blurt out a thoughtless and counterproductive response. This contributes further to the relapse. It may then become a self-reinforcing vicious circle in which each member of the family starts inadvertently feeding into another's tendency to return to old habits. Things may again start to go downhill, as if metacommunication had never happened.

Still, relapses like these are no reason to get discouraged. You can effectively address them to prevent the prior gains from unraveling, so everything you all worked so hard to change does not revert back to the way it had been. The best defense is to know that relapses are bound to happen. If you anticipate that family members might revert to old, maladaptive behavior, you should not get quite as angry when it happens as you might have otherwise.

Even if you keep your cool, wait until all of you have calmed down before addressing the relapse. Excuse yourself and exit the situation as gracefully as you can; if someone asks you why, just say you want to think about what just happened before saying anything. Waiting until cooler heads can prevail is essential; trying to discuss relapses while anyone is still angry is not going to be fruitful.

When you go off by yourself, and after you have calmed down, think about why the issue arose again in the way it did. There are two possibilities:

- Consider whether it was *you* who triggered an old pattern in *them*, because you responded in the way that their prior behavior seemed to require, even though they may not have acted exactly that way just then.

- Consider the possibility that your parents may have, without thinking, been reacting to other memories or cues in the environment—other than you—triggering their old roles.

Countermove: *Consistent Reminders of the New Path*

Once all parties have regained their composure, bring up what happened as *yet another example of the patterns you had previously discussed*, and briefly remind everybody involved about how this used to happen all the time. You can then tactfully remind the involved people about the ways all of you decided to bring a stop to the problematic patterns.

When discussing this, use the technique of apologizing for any insult or nasty remark that you may have made during the relapse *without* apologizing for how you felt. Additionally, make certain that you do not seem to be blaming anyone in particular for the relapse. You all just fell into an old habit; who started the process in any one instance is immaterial to preventing future relapses.

Talking about the incident requires, as with every interaction discussed in this book, empathic skills. Have a sense of humor and self-deprecation, as we all need to when discussing any funny human foibles—just typical screwed-up human beings doing what all of us screwed-up human beings constantly do. No big deal. No one is perfect. Finish up by asking everyone to just keep an eye out for other times and situations in which old feelings start to arise, as relapses will probably happen again.

This technique, when applied consistently, has the added benefit of making the next relapse somewhat less likely. The more you use it, the less frequent relapses become, and they eventually become very rare or may disappear altogether. But even if a relapse has not happened in a long time, remain vigilant in the now less likely case of its happening again, and if it does, do not think of it as a reason to be discouraged. You know what to do.

Natalia's Story: Falling Right Back into an Old Trap

Let us return to the case of Natalia and Stella. Their biggest issue was that both had a tendency to defend or criticize irresponsible men to the other, while switching suddenly from defense to criticism. The issue was rekindled when Stella's ex-husband, Natalia's father, tried to come back into Natalia's life after a fairly long absence. In the past, Natalia had tried to reach out to him from time to time during an estrangement; her dad would promise to show up, appear without warning maybe once, and then disappear again.

When her dad called out of the blue, Natalia was skeptical. She was afraid he was going to disappoint her again, just as he had done several previous times. On the other hand, she missed him. She nonetheless decided that her father had offered no evidence that he was going to do anything differently, so she quickly told him she would not reconnect with him unless he got therapy to help him deal with his issues.

When she told her mother about this during a routine phone call, Stella quickly jumped on Natalia's case: "Oh, come on, now! Give him a chance. He is your father, after all."

Natalia suddenly saw red. "What the hell is the matter with you?" she fumed. "There you go defending him all over again, just like you used to. Are you actually feeling sorry for him? After telling me all these years what an a-hole he actually is? Are you nuts or something?"

Natalia quickly realized what was happening. She knew she needed to stop the conversation, calm down, and discuss it later with Stella so the old battle would not continue to escalate. "I'm sorry; that was nasty of me. I'm going to hang up now so I can calm down, and we'll talk later so we can clear the air." She then hung up.

Later, she approached her mother this way: "Mom, look: I'm sorry I questioned your sanity, but I was thinking, Oh no, here we go again. But isn't it funny how we both fell right back into an old trap so quickly? We both have a soft spot in our hearts for irresponsible men, then get upset with ourselves for letting them mistreat us, but end up attacking each other over the issue instead of talking about our mutual mixed feelings. When I told you I wasn't going to put up with Dad disappointing me any more unless he got some help, we suddenly were right back where we used to be!"

Her mother smiled. "You'd think by now we would understand that we are both having the same feelings, instead of criticizing each other for having them."

"Let's try to remember to do that the next time something like this comes up."

When Problems Won't Relent

Despite your best efforts to follow this book's recommendations, sometimes the problems you've discussed keep coming up over and over again. While this can be discouraging, I still recommend that you take additional measures before deciding to keep contact to a minimum or engage in a full cutoff—measures that should only be used only as a last resort. The following suggestions have proven helpful for others in your situation.

Return to the Genogram

Ask yourself if you may have missed something when you reviewed your genogram and the family history and came up with your hypothesis about the family dynamics. Take out your family history and see if anything central has yet to be addressed. If so, repeat the steps outlined for metacommunicating with the involved parent.

Metacommunicate About Relapses

Whether or not you have found something in your review of the family history, you can bring up, as a subject for metacommunication with the relevant parents, the fact that the aggravating interactions *keep coming up*. This is similar to the strategy just recommended for bringing up a single relapse. Follow up by expressing your puzzlement over why it keeps happening, and ask what you and the parent might be able to do to resolve the issue. Invite them to review the family history with you to see if it jogs their memory so they might reveal important events about which you may still be unaware.

Seek a Therapist's Help

Consult a knowledgeable therapist for the point of view of an expert who can also be more objective than you about the dynamics that are troubling you and your family. A therapist can offer more ideas about the possible issues involved and offer additional strategies. However, be warned: these days it is becoming quite difficult to find a therapist familiar with dysfunctional family dynamics and their relationship to your internal conflicts, emotions, and cognitions.

Unfortunately, many of today's therapists seem to see all psychological problems as diseases, or look for deficiencies in their patients such as poor anger control, distorted thinking, or poor tolerance to everyday stressors. They do not address problems of family homeostasis. Their ideas can all be very invalidating to you—as if *you* are the whole problem. You can search for therapists in your city in the United States on the *Psychology Today* website ("Find a Therapist"). Their theoretical orientations are listed in their individual profiles, although they often list several of them. Before actually making an appointment, ask directly whether the therapist knows how to coach patients who are enmeshed in family dysfunction. If your whole family is willing to come for family therapy, a family systems therapist (particularly a Bowen family therapist) may be your best bet.

You can also look for family-oriented therapists who work with individuals. Bowen family therapists do work with individuals as well as with families. My own treatment paradigm, called unified therapy (Allen 1988, 1991), is not at all well known. *Interpersonal Reconstructive Therapy* (Benjamin 2006) is the closest other model to mine, but therapists who practice this one are rare as well. In the United States, the most commonly available individual therapists who deal with their clients' issues in ways somewhat similar to the ways I suggest employ schema therapy (Young et al. 2003). In the UK, the most commonly practiced recommended model is called cognitive analytic therapy (Ryle and Kerr 2001). Other relevant and helpful models include relational therapy (Wachtel 2007) and personality-guided relational psychotherapy (Magnavita 2005).

Keeping a new and improved relationship with parents who have exhibited ICDD behavior on track is a job that may never be 100-percent complete, but it does get easier over time. New habits will gradually replace the old ones and become more automatic, and relapses usually become less frequent, sometimes disappearing altogether. You can do this! It will not only lead to a more harmonious family life, but also free you to be more true to yourself so that you can follow your own muse. Because this self-actualizing process can feel unnerving at first, in the conclusion, we will look at it in a little more detail.

You Can Grow Beyond Your Parents' Limitations

After putting a stop to ICDD behavioral interactions with attachment figures—patterns that have been bothering you most of your life—you might feel pretty good about things. After all, you are no longer being invalidated or criticized, or being subjected to unreasonable demands or hateful behavior from your parents. You may feel very happy indeed. However, you might also experience a disquieting sense of unease. You may even start to experience significant anxiety and recurring episodes of low moods that do not seem to be attached to anything in particular going on in your life at that point.

This can happen because, even though you are no longer being invalidated for being the author of your own life or expressing your real feelings, you unfortunately may have been neglecting what therapists refer to as your *true self*. A paradox is at work: the type of parent-stabilizing behavior discussed in chapter 2 feels like the "real" you—even though it is essentially an act that your family dynamics have conditioned you to play. Your *false self* feels real, while your real self—the one that would have expressed itself in the absence of the family dysfunction—feels alien.

You may even start to feel like you no longer know who you are. You may not have had the time to get to know yourself completely, so you could be somewhat clueless about what you really like to do and what you want out of life. In the past, you had a set of familiar rules to follow; now that trusty framework (with all the stress and trouble it gave you) is gone.

Overcoming the Fear of Being True to You

Self-actualization means gaining the ability to be true to yourself—not just going along with everyone else's expectations of you—without impinging on other people's right to do the same. It sounds nice, but it can be quite terrifying. You now must make all the decisions about your life yourself—without any of the familiar guideposts to keep you on track. How do you even know what is right for you? What if you make a bad choice? You will need to take full responsibility!

There are no rules or guidelines on how to behave in every situation that apply specifically to you or to any other single individual. Possibly for the first time in your life, you are more or less on your own. Even if your family is now supportive of your independence instead of abandoning you when you break free of their confining rules, this highly uncomfortable feeling persists. You might even be tempted to go back to your old dysfunctional ways just because they are familiar to you and are therefore more comfortable. The loss of familiarity with the world around you may plunge you into an odd sort of mourning state. You now realize you have spent a good portion of your life living in a way that has brought you considerable pain. What a waste! You can never get that time back. The old adage about today being the first day of the rest of your life may bring little comfort.

While there is no quick and easy way to make these sorts of feelings—which together are referred to as "groundlessness" by some therapists—go away, they *will*; you *can* get past it. It is something you just need to tolerate until it goes away. It helps to know that what you are experiencing is a normal reaction and that it even has a name. Nothing is wrong with you.

So how do you get to know yourself better? The work you can do on self-actualization, described in the next section, can help speed up the process.

EXERCISE: Explore Beyond Old Limitations

Review the ways you have reacted to your parents' behaviors. Return to the exercises in chapters 1 and 2 that helped you identify how your life has been shaped and limited by your parents' dysfunction and needs. Ask yourself:

- How was I affected by their need for me to follow old, outdated family rules?

- What areas of my life were most affected by my attempts to stabilize my parents?

- Was my choice of relationships limited?

- Did it affect my professional life or career?

- Do I have hobbies or interests that I might have pursued if my parents hadn't discouraged me?

Write down the answers in an uninhibited, freeform way. Let yourself explore you.

Self-Actualization: Getting to Know Yourself

The role that you previously played in order to stabilize your family has probably interfered to a greater or lesser degree with many different facets of your life. You may have had to limit your choices in romantic partners, careers, relationships with extended family, and recreation. As you go through this section, keep in mind all the ways and the circumstances in which your having tried to placate your parents has monopolized your time.

Romantic Relationships

Ask yourself whether all your romantic partners have some peculiarities in common. Did you, for instance, get involved with a series of "fixer-uppers" who all had major issues with which you would try to help them, finding yourself bored by more put-together partners? Did you pick partners who dominated you in unproductive ways? Who were far more or far less adventurous than you, or consistently enmeshed or distant from their own parents? Loners or people pleasers?

If this has been the case, do not jump into a new relationship until you have started to date a variety of other types of people with different behavior and attitudes in terms of potential CCRTs. Consider the "program of threes" recommended by Kirschner and Kirschner (1986). They believe you should not think about settling down in an exclusive relationship with anybody until you have dated at least three completely different types of potential partners. Do not discourage yourself by employing your old defenses, such as thinking that better partners do not exist or that there are no ways nowadays to meet a variety of new people. There are dating sites online, dating services, and classes and group functions of various interest groups (see the discussion of Meetup.com in the upcoming section on hobbies and personal passions) that you can attend in which you can meet new people. If someone appears to be a good fit before you have dated others, you can still date them, but hold off on making it an exclusive relationship.

Another important task is for you to become aware of, and learn to identify and pay attention to, the red flags in potential romantic partners indicating big problems that you may have previously ignored when you met somebody new. Avoid people who seem to exhibit these characteristics. When there's a potential for major

CCRTs, better to err on the side of being a little too picky than not being picky enough. Most people who repeatedly get involved with the same type of problematic person really do notice the red flags at the beginning of those relationships, but they often deny this fact to themselves. Which ones do you need to look out for? Now is the time to start paying closer attention to those flags. They are usually not all that subtle.

Dorion's Story: Familiar Red Flags

Dorion had successfully negotiated more space from his overbearing mother. When he looked at his relationships, he realized he had been repeatedly involved with women who seemed overly dependent on their mothers. Realizing this, he began to make point of looking very closely at the relationship that a potential partner had with her mother, seeking signs of entanglement and unnecessary caretaking in either direction. If he saw that, he knew he should resist the temptation to get involved with that woman.

Other Family Relationships

Ask yourself how your parents have affected your relationships with your siblings, aunts, uncles, cousins, or in-laws. How do you *really* feel about the idea of close family gatherings for birthdays, graduations, and holidays—assuming, of course, that old ICDD behaviors would not arise? If you would like to have a relationship with relatives who were formerly off limits due to your parents' objections, will you now have to deal with the aftermath of your parents' previous efforts to subvert your relationship with those relatives through maneuvers such as gossip?

If those were major CCRTs for your problematic parents in the past, ideally your efforts to follow the strategies in this book mean such parental interference has now stopped, but you may nonetheless have some repair work to do to reestablish better relationships. Even if, say, a sibling did not require a detriangulation effort on your part before you confronted your parents, you might need to go back and include the same metacommunicative techniques and strategies outlined in this book to try to establish closer relationships with that sibling.

Kingston's Story: Reconnecting with an Exiled Uncle

Kingston's father had almost never spoken of, let alone spoke to, his twin brother. Whenever Kingston asked his father about him, his mother would create a big fuss as a distraction. If Kingston mentioned calling him, his mother would become very disturbed, but would never say why.

When putting his family's genogram together, Kingston decided to defy his parents. Without telling them, he contacted his uncle. After finally learning the reasons for his father's falling out with his sibling, he was able to successfully empathize with both his parents in their feelings about him while informing his parents that the estranged sibling had been happy to hear from him and that he had enjoyed talking to him. He let his parents know that he planned to maintain occasional contact, adding that he hoped they would not continue to view that as a personal betrayal.

Career and Professional Life

You also need to ask yourself about any career aspirations you may once have had but felt forced to abandon due to family pressure. Have you felt stuck in a job you despise? Could you really do—or begin learning to do—something else? Or have you been jumping from job to job because you feared success?

Children are often asked what they want to be when they grow up, and their answers often reveal their real interests. Although very young kids may have unrealistic, romanticized ideas about livelihoods, older kids may have thought more realistically about career options. They are often less inhibited in thinking about their likes and dislikes than they might be when they get to be adults. I suggest thinking back to when you were younger and someone asked you what you wanted to do. How did you respond? Your answers may give you clues about what you might like even now, although you have become conditioned to avoid it or have been invalidated for trying to achieve certain goals later on in life.

Another avenue for self discovery in this arena is going to the library or doing searches on the Internet and reading about various jobs. Let your mind and fingers wander freely. Do any sound interesting? Do any sound like fun? Even if they require training, is it possible you could go back to school? Or is there something similar that you might be able to do without a lot of additional training? Some workplaces will train you on the job. I also suggest reading everything you can get your hands on about the best way to conduct yourself in a job interview, and how to best explain to a potential employer any big gaps in your resume if you were a caretaker for your parents.

Troy's Story: No Longer Fearing Success

Troy had dreamed of being a lawyer; as a teen, he had obsessively watched TV shows and movies about criminal defense attorneys. This ambition was derailed because, throughout his childhood, both parents constantly told him that he was not "college material" and should instead go to trade school and become a plumber. So that was what he did, seemingly forgetting about his former plans. However, he felt stifled, bored, and unfulfilled in his job. This prompted him to confront his parents over their apparent lack of confidence in him, and after following the steps recommended in this book, he was finally able to enroll in college despite some lingering feelings of low self-confidence.

Hobbies and Personal Passions

Again, ask yourself what you liked to do when you were younger. What was fun? What new things that you've never even thought about before come to your mind? Which favorite activities may have fallen by the wayside while you were preoccupied with and dominated by your parents' ICDD behavior? Have you addressed those specific behaviors with them in the ways recommended in this book? If not, you may have some additional metacommunication to do.

Pick a few pursuits you have never tried before and that do not require a long or expensive period of training, and *try them on for size*. Not sure how? I suggest a website called Meetup.com, which lists a variety of local groups interested in various activities that have regular meetings of people who share those interests. These groups are often very inexpensive. You might want to try, say, politics by getting involved with the party of your choice. You can find groups of people who like books, puzzles, wine-tasting, playing bridge, a local sports team; the list goes on and on. If you find that whatever you try is just not your cup of tea, do not get discouraged. Try something else.

EXERCISE: What Will Your Life Look Like?

With the goal of achieving whatever level of success you can in reducing or putting a stop to the parental behavior that has gotten in the way of your following your dreams or having more satisfying relationships, you now can go on to outline any potential concrete changes you'll then want to make in your life.

- How close will you be with your parents and other family members?

- Are you going to need strict boundaries with them in terms of limiting your time together or which subjects you are willing to discuss with them?

- Which choices do you think you will want to make about areas over which family members are conflicted?

- Where do you really stand on matters such as religion, politics, social class, or sexual morality, and do you want any of your current stances to change?

All of these are important questions, so devote ample time to journaling on each of these topics. As you do so, let your mind roam freely, without censoring or automatically dismissing *any* thoughts that emerge. Write them all down. Read and reread what comes out. Down deep, you know what really excites or entertains you and what you find uninteresting or unappealing. Continue to look inward, even if at first it seems like you are studying an alien from another planet.

Becoming self-actualized while remaining in contact with a warm and supportive family can be one of life's greatest joys, but it remains somewhat elusive for many people and their families. As we have seen, people can become stuck operating with group rules that may have made sense in the past but no longer work, and that induce in children self-defeating and self-destructive roles and patterns of behavior. My hope is that you have learned techniques from this book that allow you to escape from those old rules and patterns so that you become all you can be—and all you wish to be—without having to lose family ties in the process.

You have learned about the reasons for dysfunctional family patterns, including the importance of attachment behavior, kin selection, family homeostasis, and intrapsychic conflicts generated by rapid changes in ethnic and cultural norms. You have learned how to research the events and personalities in your family's historical background and to form hypotheses that help you to understand how CCRTs emerge.

I hope you have used this book to learn metacommunicative strategies that enable you to speak up in empathic ways, stand up for yourself, and say what you really think without worrying about being invalidated by parents you know and care about. In turn, I hope this has allowed you to abandon needlessly angry, anxious, or self-sacrificial behavior that, while well meant and effective at stabilizing your family in the short run, backfires in the long run by preventing effective problem solving.

I wish you all the best as you proceed with putting all you have learned into practice, both to forge new family understanding and to enrich your own life through self-actualization. A far more satisfying and fulfilling life awaits you.

Acknowledgments

I began writing this book following an inquiry from the man who became my acquisitions editor at New Harbinger Publications, Ryan Buresh. He contacted me after reading one of my posts on my blog at *Psychology Today*. His input and suggestions have been indispensible. He, and the entire team at New Harbinger, basically provided me with a detailed tutorial on how to write an accessible and comprehensible self-help book for lay readers, and for that I am deeply indebted to them. Thanks especially to Vicraj Gill for her impressive hard work—she provided me with amazingly intricate feedback on the first two drafts of the manuscript—and for the spot-on help in fine tuning the book provided by Jennifer Holder at Fullbloom Publications and by copyeditor Kristi Hein.

I am grateful to the editor of my blog at *Psychology Today*, Lybi Ma, who, after finding and reading some of the posts on my other blog (*Family Dysfunction and Mental Health*), invited me to be a contributor to her far more widely followed publication.

Additionally, thanks to Dr. Susan Heitler, a fellow member of the Society for the Exploration of Psychotherapy Integration (SEPI)—an academic group attempting to integrate the various schools of thought within psychotherapy—for her suggestions as well as for writing the foreword to this book.

I would also like to acknowledge the marketing team at New Harbinger for their unusual efforts to make sure this book finds the people who might benefit from it.

A special thank-you goes to the scores of scientists and psychotherapists whose work has inspired my thinking over my long career, especially the late Murray Bowen—a pioneer in family systems psychotherapy and the multigenerational model of family dysfunction—and Edward O. Wilson, the person most responsible for our understanding of the importance of group dynamics in evolution.

And finally, I send my deepest appreciation for the unwavering support and understanding of the love of my life, my wife, Harriet.

References

Alberti, R., and Emmons, M. 2017. *Your Perfect Right*. 10th ed. San Luis Obispo, CA: Impact.

Allen, D. M. 1988. *A Family Systems Approach to Individual Psychotherapy*. Northvale, NJ: Jason Aronson. First published 1988 as *Unifying Individual and Family Therapies* by Jossey-Bass (San Francisco).

Allen, D. M. 1991. *Deciphering Motivation in Psychotherapy*. New York: Plenum Publishers.

Allen, D. M. 2003. *Psychotherapy with Borderline Patients: An Integrated Approach*. Mahweh, NJ: Lawrence Erlbaum.

Allen, D. M., Abramson, H., Whitson, S., Al-Taher, M., Morgan, S., Veneracion-Yumul, A., Kondam, S., Goswami, Y., and Mason, M. 2005. "Perceptions of Contradictory Communication from Parental Figures by Adults with Borderline Personality Disorder: A Preliminary Study." *Comprehensive Psychiatry* 46 (5): 340–352.

Barrett, M., and Trepper, T. 1992. "Unmasking the Incestuous Family." *The Family Therapy Networker*, May-June: 39–46.

Benjamin, L. S. 2005. *Interpersonal Reconstructive Therapy*. New York: Guilford Press.

Bowen, M. 1978. *Family Therapy in Clinical Practice*. New York: Jason Aronson.

Bowlby, J. 1988. "Developmental Psychiatry Comes of Age." *American Journal of Psychiatry* 145 (1): 1–10.

Boyd-Franklin, N. 1989. *Black Families in Therapy: A Multisystems Approach.* New York: Guilford Press.

Brothers, L. 1989. "A Biological Perspective on Empathy." *American Journal of Psychiatry* 146 (1): 10–19.

Cohen, D. 2013. *Family Secrets: Shame and Privacy in Modern Britain.* New York: Oxford University Press.

Eagleman, D. 2015. *The Brain with David Eagleman.* PBS television series.

Fromm, E. 1969. *Escape from Freedom.* New York: Avon Books. First published 1941.

Gilbert, R. 1992. *Extraordinary Relationships: A New Way of Thinking About Human Interactions.* Minneapolis, MN: Chronimed.

Heffernan, M. 2011. *Willful Blindness: Why We Ignore the Obvious at Our Peril.* New York: Bloomsbury.

Henriques, G. 2011. *A New Unified Theory of Psychology.* New York: Springer.

Kirschner, D. A., and Kirschner, S. 1986. *Comprehensive Family Therapy.* New York: Brunner, Mazel.

Lau, A., McCabe, K., Yeh, M., Garland, A., Wood, P., and Hough, L. 2005. "The Acculturation Gap-Distress Hypothesis Among High-Risk Mexican American Families." *Journal of Family Psychology* (193): 367–375.

Lott, D. A. 2003. "Unlearning Fear: Calcium Channel Blockers and the Process of Extinction." *Psychiatric Times* May: 9–12.

Luborsky, L., and Crits-Christoph, P. 1990. *Understanding Transference: The CCRT Method.* New York: Basic Books.

Magnavita, J. J. 2005. *Personality-Guided Relational Psychotherapy.* Washington, DC: American Psychological Association.

McGoldrick, M., Pearce, J. K., and Giordano, J., eds. 2005. *Ethnicity and Family Therapy.* 3rd ed. New York: Guilford Press.

Ryle, A. and Kerr, I. B. 2001. *Introduction to Cognitive-Analytic Therapy: Principles and Practice.* New York: Wiley.

Sapolsky, R. 2017. *Behave: The Biology of Humans at Our Best and Worst.* New York: Penguin Press.

Slipp, S. 1984. *Object Relations: A Dynamic Bridge Between Individual and Family Treatment.* New York: Jason Aronson.

Tan, C. 2012. *Search Inside Yourself: The Unexpected Path to Achieving Success, Happiness, and World Peace.* New York: HarperOne.

Wachtel, P. L. 2007. *Relational Theory and the Practice of Psychotherapy.* New York: Guilford Press.

Watzlawick, P., Beavin, J., and Jackson, D. 1967. *Pragmatics of Human Communication.* New York: Norton.

Wile, D. 1981. *Couples Therapy: A Nontraditional Approach.* New York: Wiley.

Wilson, E. O. 1998. *Consilience: The Unity of Knowledge.* New York: Alfred A. Knopf.

Young, J., Klosko, J., and Weishaar, M. 2003. *Schema Therapy: A Practitioner's Guide.* New York: Guilford Press.

David M. Allen, MD, is professor emeritus of psychiatry and former director of psychiatric residency training at the University of Tennessee Health Science Center in Memphis, TN. He is author of the book *How Dysfunctional Families Spur Mental Disorders*. He has carried out research on personality disorders, is a psychotherapy theorist, and is former associate editor of the *Journal of Psychotherapy Integration*. He is also author of three books for psychotherapists, as well as numerous journal articles and book chapters.

Foreword writer **Susan Heitler, PhD**, is a clinical psychologist whose publications—including *The Power of Two* and *The Power of Two Workbook*—have become classics in their fields. Heitler is a graduate of Harvard University and earned her doctorate from New York University.

MORE BOOKS *from*
NEW HARBINGER PUBLICATIONS

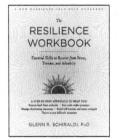
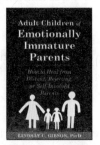
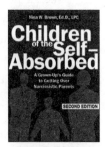

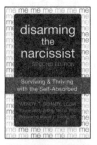